Seductive Aesthetics of Postcolonialism

CRITICAL BODIES
Joseph J. Pilotta, *series editor*

The Body in Human Inquiry: Interdisciplinary Explorations of Embodiment
Vincente Berdayes, Luigi Esposition, and John W. Murphy (eds.)

Knowledge and the Production of Non-knowledge: An Exploration of Alien
Mythology in Post-War America
Mark Featherstone

The New Age Ethic and the Spirit of Postmodernity
Carmen Kuhling

Abjection and Correction in Ethnographic Studies: Communication Issues in
the Cultural Tourism of Isla Mujeres, Mexico
Jill Adair McCaughan

Seductive Aesthetics of Postcolonialism
Rekha Menon

Plato's Cave: Television and its Discontents (rev. ed.)
John O'Neill

Why I Still Want My MTV
Kevin Williams

forthcoming

Phenomenology, Body Politics, and the Future of Communication Theory
Hwa Kol Jung (ed.)

Hispanic Tele-visions
Elizabeth Lozano

Body Works: Essays on Modernity and Morality
John O'Neill

The Philosophy of Frank Herbert's Dune
Kevin Williams

Seductive Aesthetics of Postcolonialism

REKHA MENON

Berklee College of Music

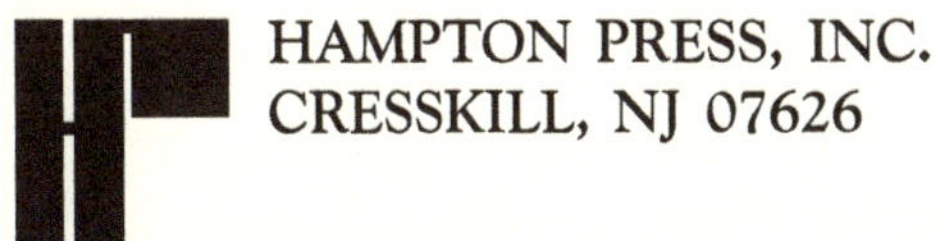

HAMPTON PRESS, INC.
CRESSKILL, NJ 07626

Printed in the United States of America

Library of Congress Cataloging-in-Publication Data

Menon, Rekha.
    Seductive aesthetics of postcolonialism / Rekha Menon. — 1st ed.
        p. cm. — (Hampton Press communication series. Critical bodies)
    Includes bibliographical references and indexes.
    ISBN 978-1-57273-972-7 (hardbound) — ISBN 978-1-57273-973-4 (pbk.)
    1. Postcolonialism and the arts—India. I. Title.
    NX180.P67M46 2010
    700.954—dc22   2010018446

Hampton Press, Inc.
23 Broadway
Cresskill, NJ 07626

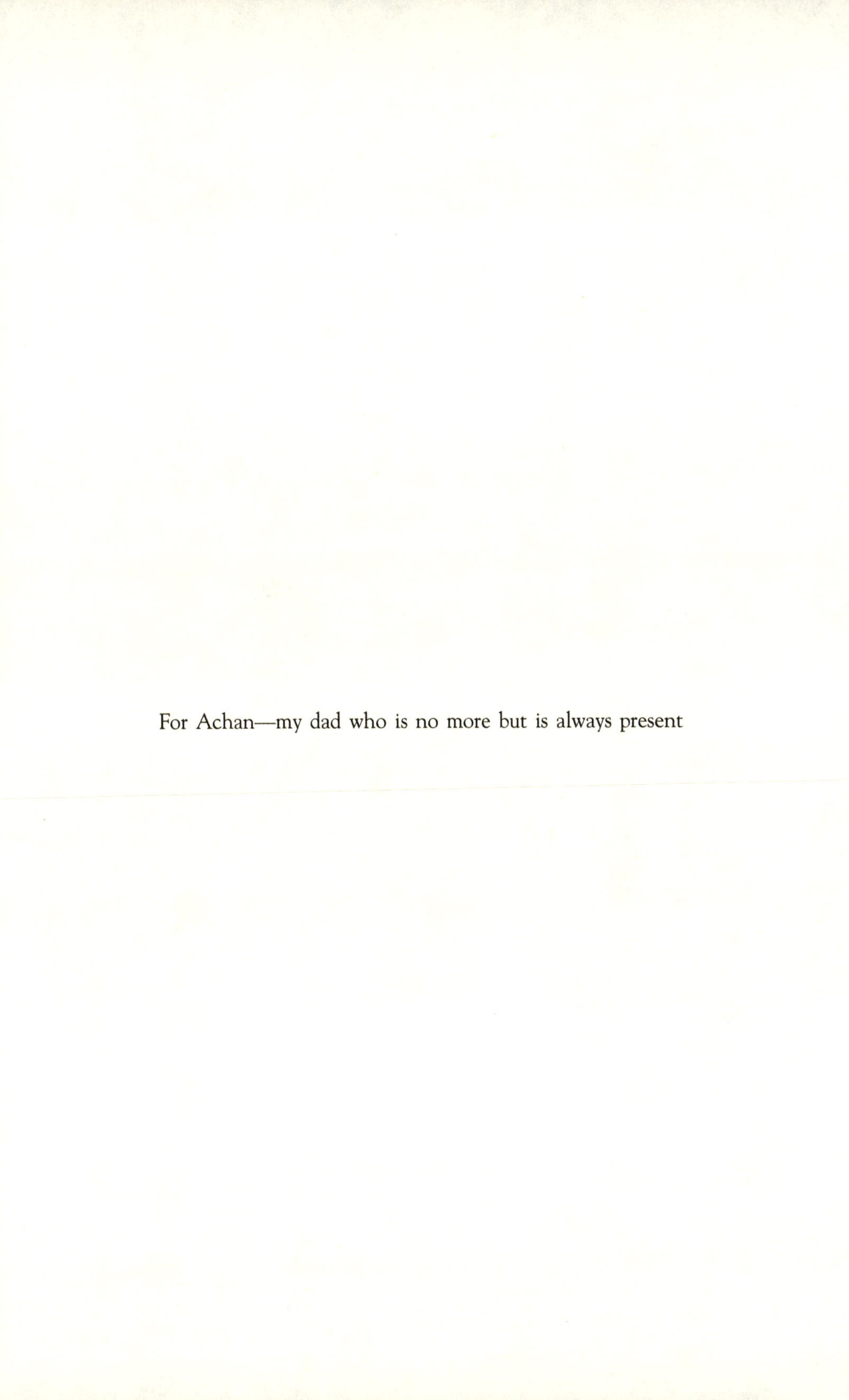

For Achan—my dad who is no more but is always present

Contents

Preface   ix

Acknowledgments   xi

Introduction   1
    Between the Legs The Space   8

RE-DRESS COSMOS   9

1. Disrobing and Redressing   11
    Excess of Judgments   11
    West Casting a Shadow of Morals   12
    The Transgression of Limitation of the Cosmic Presence   12
    Trendy Exoticism   17
    Cosmic Eroticism Dressed in Moral Space   19
    Who Are We?   36

INSCRIPTIVE SEDUCTION   39

2. Transgressions: Redressing Tradition   41
    Disruption of Traditional Other   48
    The Scars of the Past   56

VACILLATING MORALITY   57

3. Desirous Seduction   59
    The Irony of Desirous Seduction in Bollywood Films   59
    The Globalization of Indian Marriages   66
    Death of Knowing   73

EMBRACING THE SATIATE SPACE　75

Afterword　89
　　Liberated or Trapped: Third World's Third World Dreamings　89
　　How Many Footsteps　91

Notes　97

Bibliography　103

Author Index　113

Subject Index　115

Preface

Voices I Hear...

If you had a Brown/Black face and a strange sounding name, You had little right to be here. . . .

Spoke a different tongue, though I am well versed in your tongue, do you have the right to teach and be here. . . .

Do you have a right to flaunt your strange, immoral, erotic art??????

And nefariously spread the exotic culture in the face of the majority population. . . .

But for the Seduction . . .

The spicy hot exotic flavors

The bright colors

The sinuous erotica

Dark forces of Exotica

YOU are not listening to me, REKHA . . .

Do you understand?

(Here I am why is she repeating. . . .

I am not a dumb Indian, for pete's sake, I do understand English; I teach in English. . . .

I feel like crying out: You know we were colonized, I think, feel, read and write in English. . . .)

Acknowledgments

The successful completion of this manuscript has been largely possible because of Barbara Bernstein, president/publisher, Hampton Press and Sue Morreale; they were very diligent in editing and in the layout of the text. I thank them for their patience and support. I would like to thank Prof. Joseph J. Pilotta for giving me the opportunity to publish in his series "Critical Bodies." I thank Prof. Jeffner Allen, for her continuous encouragement, valuable comments, support, interest and help at various stages, which enabled me to complete this manuscript. I will always be grateful and indebted to her. I thank Kaylene Waite and Chee-Ping Ho, for helping me with the scanning of the visual images. I would like to thank the artists and the galleries for being very generous in providing and giving me permission to reproduce the visual images. I thank State University of New York, Buffalo State for the individual development grant/award (while I was tenured at SUNY, Buffalo State). The grant helped in the completion of my research for this manuscript. No words are enough to thank my mentor Prof. Algis Mickunas, whose passion and guidance led me out of hurdles of my colonial self. I could not have hoped to complete this work without his teaching, inspiration, passion for the cosmic sense and his overarching support, admiration and interest in my work. I am grateful and will hold the utmost respect for Prof. Algis Mickunas who played a great role in shaping my life and in bringing me to where I am. Finally, all people who shaped my life, my parents, sisters, deserve my greatest respect, and my husband and son for their love and patience towards ME—an 'In-Between Self.'

Introduction

"Do I have to change me "I" to be loved by you, "the Other"

"How hard it is for us to think we the Other can choose to become writers, philosophers, artists, much less think, feel and believe that we the Other can,"[1] *and that we are.*

Writing through my body, the body wrote itself. Yet, we the Other to the West do not have bodies as our properties, we are our bodies, and we are ourselves only while being in our world.[2] Our body as the Other was stripped, reduced to the cultural possession and clothed in the discourse of the victor. Can one recloth the texture of our body, my skin or shall we, and I, wear it with the marks inscribed by the Other? The book adroitly refers and relates to aesthetics, gender, money, power, possession, politics, difference, justice, as they are played out on the body of the Other. The body becomes a battleground, especially the body of the Other, where the sadistic utility, pleasures, are pitted against the worldly passions of the Other. This leads to the notion that because the body is coextensive with the environment (a being in the world), then through the body the environment is controlled, subjected, and mastered so that the Other becomes objectified as an aspect of reduced environment for utility. It is placed in a subordinate position and pushed to the demonic netherworld, or hyperexoticized and touristically consumed.

Colonization is a practice of theft, including the theft of bodies. Can the ones who are colonized reclaim their traditional bodies, to acquire ownership of them, to redress them in their once dynamic, erotic attire? The body is a highly contested site of knowledge and power, a property to be possessed and utilized. The politics played during the colonial period in India has carved imprints on Indian bodies, disrobing and degrading the cultural values and practices and stripping them of their discursive practices, regarding them as the weaker sex, shameless, and naked. The erotic world, erotic expressivity, aesthetics were pushed aside and robbed of its fire, allurement, and passion. The lived worldly passions were and are questioned, and replaced by moralized sexed bodies. The colonizers and the colonized neocolonials were subjected to conventions and attires fit for consumption by mass gaze. This volume explores and discusses the reduction of the Other as a sexual object, where the Other is stripped of one's worldly passions only to be placed in the realm of the immoral. The Other is alluring, seductive but offensive and thus should be relegated to the bin of primitivism or savagely capitalized as touristic exotica.

All aspects of the colonized culture have been and continue to be regarded as "primitive and immoral" and morality was interpreted purely sexually—nevertheless they were seductive and exotic. In this sense, the actions and images of divinities, their aesthetics were immoral because ultimately they had to be defined sexually. Arts were immoral, because they had *kamic*, eros, desire, passion forces, which had to be understood sexually. Because the colonized people were purely sexual, and at the same time seductive, they then had something feminine about them, something alluring and offensive, and hence had to be attacked and destroyed in their sexuality and above all in their eroticism. This is the sadistic reduction of Indian cultural aspects to sexed bodies and their parts and such parts must be sodomized not for productivity but for Eve's creation, disembodiment. I recently visited London, looking around, the ugliness, dirt and dour mood was overwhelming (my opinion). I wondered about this is the country—the Empire, the Brits who colonized India. It reminded me of the British writings describing India and its "dirtiness." Most likely the British attempted to hide their own condition (after all during the time of colonialism London was a place of squalor, torture, poverty, indentured servants and sour smelling aristocrats) and imposed it on Others, allowing them to see themselves as "clean," "divine" and the Others as dirty and demonic. I was convinced they were afraid of the Other's beauty and desired the Other, so the only way to hide their fear and consume their desire was to push the Other to the demonic, nether-realm.

Deprived of its home both in terms of space and time, the colonized became a reflected image in the multiple mirrors of European civilization. In this book, I reflect on British colonization of India, which was not merely confined to a territorial space, but also colonized India's sense of time and being. India's present became regarded as corruption of the past, a past that was glorious but could only be recovered via the European present. This was the notion of the colonizers and the colonized in some instances:

> To Marx, it was a moribund culture of outlived feudalism seething with savage gods and dark superstitions. To Hegel, Indian thought was reduced to an abstract dream image, never reaching the level of philosophy which was regarded as an uniquely European achievement. For European merchants, conquerors, India was an object of desire.... For Husserl and Heidegger it was in Europe alone where they saw the power for the appropriation, actualization and rebirth of India's past. India's present would have any meaning if only it could be recast in the ideal image of Europe.[3]

Such was the idealized image of Europe presented to the Indians, and at that time for Indians, Europe was the epitome and the pinnacle of human civilization both in the sphere of material progress and intellectual achievements. As one of the Bengali intelligentsia states in 19th century, "never before has the world witnessed such material progress as has been achieved by the civilization of modern Europe, nor had the earlier generations of mankind hoped for such progress."[4] This sums up some of the Indian intelligentsia's reaction to Europe.

The adulation and splendor, though, was reduced to spiritual desolation and economic penury and the traditional learning was gradually replaced by the European system of education, with English as a compulsory language of the medium of instruction, of which India is still a victim today. Nevertheless, I will say that I grew up learning English and I am writing my book in English, the colonizer's language, but it is too late to back out, and thus I cherish this language and I do not fret about it. The famous Raja Ram Mohan Roy, who was a learned Hindu steeped in his traditional self, was, at the same time, totally overwhelmed with his encounter with Europe. He was one of the "first Indian modernists who saw in these Western institutions the source of enlightenment which would bring Indians out of darkness of their superstitions."[5] Although this was the view of some of the Hindu intelligensia, such a view was not enlightening to the sensitive middle class of India. The middle class viewed the English as materialistic, grabbing other people's territory and property, and thus they had to be looked upon with resentment and bitterness. At the same time, there was the extraordinary cultural phenomenon which was called the Bengal renaissance, "it was nothing else but the massive intellectual endeavor on the part of the Hindus to respond and relate to Europe in order to redefine their past and assert national identity."[6] Thus, all these Indians encountered the British with different modes: to cherish, like the traditionalist looked at the British to glorify his past, or the patriot who affirmed his nationalism or the nationalist intellectual who emphasized the secular nature of his Vedic heritage.[7]

Thus, Indians, for the first time, faced the presence of an alien culture. Unlike the Muslims who could be effectively ignored as simply another religion, it was the British enlightened rationalism and material advancement that posed a challenge. It created an ambiguity of being attracted and repelled at the same time. I feel it is the same with the globalizing logic today in which we are all caught up, where we are attracted and repelled by global logic at the same time. Thus, there was a strange situation where two cultures were trapped together, bound, and bewitched by one another, from which there was no escape. I agree with what Nirad Chaudhari said about the British: although they ruled India for so long they failed to strike roots in India, and they were different from Islam:

> While Islam could never overcome its 'otherness' in the Hindu framework
> of life, it gradually got itself 'Indianized' and felt at home in India and
> stopped looking back at its foreign roots. On the other hand the British

never forgot their otherness. They always had to stress their otherness as outsiders, as representatives of a superior race and advanced civilization.[8]

But they did feel strange in a country whose climate was detestable for them and whose customs they could not comprehend. Although the British had the authority and power, they still did feel strange and ill-at-ease in India. And yet, they were fascinated and attracted by the exotica, the aesthetic allurements, the erotic "immorality," which they tried to reject, and yet to which, by their very insistent rejections, they revealed their attraction.

In turn, the English did penetrate deeply into the psyche of India. The result was that people were Hindu by birth, yet English by education. This means that they were essentially accepting the Europeanized ideals of historical progress. This led to acceptance of the self-image of Europe as the ideal image of humanity itself. In turn, this led the enlightened Hindus to revise their version of the traditional conception of the self. Where the self, *atman*, was part of the mirror image of the *parmatma*, now that self became a subself, reduced to a minor accessory of a larger reality, not of the *Brahman*, but of the history of the image of European man.[9] Thus, the enlightened Indians, including Vivekananda, saw the Indian self from the western gaze, "a puny little wretched thing shivering in the darkness; not the awakened *atman* of *Gita* but the maggot rotting in the putrid flesh of a backward tradition."[10] This step was the final version of the British: to colonize the Indians by stripping them of their self and replacing it with another self. This is one major sense of saying that the self of the traditional Indian was naked and had to acquire the clothing of the modern British self disrobing the Indian cosmic *atman*, self.

One was invited by the colonizing acts to join a circle of self-interpretation that included all the terms of progress, history, reason, enlightenment, and civilization. And yet, the Indian self could never be completely colonized, and hence, subsumed under this circle. After all, even the British, despite their aloof rejection, were attracted and incorporated, at least in part, in the Indian tradition. The identity of Hindu, unlike the British, never resided in the self as an autonomous entity, but in the larger pattern of beliefs of *Dharma*. This was the dilemma that existed during the time of the British. The Westernized Indian reformers found the European ideals of humanism very enamoring, but they could not accept them totally. They saw no harmonization between the European ideals and the Hindu concept of *Dharma*. It was a confrontation in which one was "seeking salvation, *moksha*, through performing ones' obligation and the other was seeking power by asserting its freedom sanctioned and sanctified by history."[11] These are some of the examples of how a colonial civilization distorts or elevates its own image by casting a shadow between itself and the eye of the receiving subject. As the Indian was historicized in the British context, he was de-Indianized in the context of his own traditional self, even if not completely.

With the rise of salvational belief in the powers of science and rational knowledge, the implicit faith of the Hindu in the rites and rituals, in the network of myths and symbols, that constituted his or her *dharma* through which he or she deciphered and interpreted the text of the world, was seriously undermined. The social situation of the Hindu self was distorted seriously and its *raison d'être* was radically transformed:

> The European colonization cast a shadow, a cleavage right in the middle of the Indian consciousness. Tradition, which was a way of life, was external-ized as something belonging to the past, and Europe, which was an external factor, was internalized as an iron in the soul. Not merely that it was iron in whose mold India was supposed to cast her own future destiny.[12]

India looked towards Europe for achieving material progress and towards its own tradition for salvation, *moksha*. This kind of an Indian psyche had totally opposed directions that could not be bridged, even to this day.

Vivekananda's words, for example note, that, "the only way, in his view, by which India could come out of darkness was to inculcate that quality of masculine vigor and dynamism that fascinated him in the European character; like many of his Westernized contemporaries he saw no contradiction in the fact that what he most admired of the West, was rational positivism and male aggressiveness."[13] It did not even strike Vivekananda that this was the main incursion of the colonizer to disrupt the Indian society, which he deeply admired and wanted to preserve. Vivekananda's response was a despairing attempt to seek an answer from a tradition that could, at the same time, be acceptable to his rationalist mind, thereby redeeming him from existential angst. Yet Vivekananda seemed to overlook that this angst itself was a very Europeanized rational product that he did not want to abandon, "it was like seeking relief from the disease by which one was afflicted."[14]

This was the state of the Hindus who were caught up on the one side with European rationalism in their hands and, on the other, with their tra-ditional self. They faced this predicament, which was very painful and, in a way, uprooting from one's own tradition and alienating from one's self. The Indian modernizers were caught in a contradiction from which they could never escape: uprooted from their tradition they had to seek for a rejuvena-tion of the self only in Europe; and this could only be done by assimilating oneself with the British as if surrendering oneself. But, the assimilation could never be possible, for the British never accepted the Indians. They were always looked upon as the aliens with a past, primitive, uncivilized tradition, and, in this way, the modern Indians became the Other. Thus, the mark of being the Other was always present in the gaze of the British, by which we are marked even today.

The cleavage that the British had introduced in the Indian consciousness, one part submerged in tradition and the other trying to cast itself in the image of the European man, generated a kind of bad faith which was suffered by the traditional Hindus and also the modern Hindu reformers.[15] At the same time that the traditionalists asserted their past, the Hindu modernizers tried to get rid of bad faith by becoming more British than the British themselves. This class of people later became influential in the Indian national movement to seek independence. The cleavage caused by the British for India by this encounter was like a crack in the mirror: one part reflecting the glorified image of the past and the other reflecting on the image of Europe to serve as a model.[16] The Indian "renaissance," as it was called, was both a reflection of the Hindu consciousness of the self, as well as its estrangement.[17] A space was thereby created between the two traditions, the Indian and the British, within which, "the voice of one evokes a responsive echo in the other, feeling the deprivation of one's own through the longings of the other."[18] This space, which was created during the British colonization, still remains as a space, a between space of two different cultures trying to create a mediated space, the in-between common space.

I see White supremacy as an entire world that found its power over the Other. The Other had to be diminished in body and color: inferior, dirty, uncivilized, primitive, immoral. In this context, the hermenuetics of the Other as negative and lacking is established on the basis of the logic of Westernization. Only in terms of this logic does the Indian, the Other, have to become a lesser being, not a civilized head, but an unwashed bottom. As Derrida states, "metaphysics is the White mythology which resembles and reflects the culture of the West: the White man takes his own mythology, Indo European mythology, his own logos, that is, the mythos of his idiom, for the universal form and calls it Reason."[19] It is with this mythos that the White man dismisses the Other; yet, the Other, too, starts considering the White mythos as the universal Reason, enlightened mythos. This very mythos, which was considered by the West as the powers of rationality, made the Other feel that to be modern, enlightened, to free himself, he had to incorporate this instrumental device in order to dominate himself and perhaps, even, the European. Foucault was right in saying that this "reason is a despotic enlightenment."[20] Reason is an enlightened hegemony, similar to political hegemony. As Levinas argues, the "ontological imperialism" occurs when the Other is neutralized by a means of encompassing, that is, when the relation with the Other is accomplished through its assimilation, political implications of which are clear into the self, and then the alterity of the Other vanishes.[21]

If I continue to discuss the Other in terms of European scholars, I construct the Other to the terms of the colonizer's own self-image, as the self consolidated Other. I give preeminence to the authority of European scholars and the assumed primacy of the category of the West that establishes Europe's Other as a narcissistic self-image. The scholars just mentioned discuss and endorse the political project of establishing forms of knowledge of the Other. Yet, this immense domain of practice, the epiphany of triumphant reason, deciphers the Other in the historical transcendental framework of the West.[22] In this sense, European theorists have had the same time scheme, with a strict chronology and a location for every phenomenon, regardless of the subject matter. Although Foucault and Derrida try to dehistoricize the lives of humans, and analyze discursive systems, they still fall into the trap of dehistoricizing humanity from Western history and its subject. Hence, their episteme still belongs to the West and blinds the history of the Other.

The understanding of the Other is relevant for art/aesthetics because the West judge art in terms of their context of understanding. There are various theories of art, ranging from the notion of art for art's sake, to art as a copy of "reality," all the way to art as artifacts that are regarded as socially functional but have no designation as art. Africans, in many cases, did not call their creative productions "art." My concern is to articulate a relationship between art/aesthetics and the Other. To accomplish this task, I propose a "logic" that first establishes the "Other" as of different race, and as a result, as in some senses inadequate, less than the "real human," and perhaps even morally deficient. For this "logic" I fall prey to some of Sartre's notions, such as bad faith, objectification of the Other, and the tension between sadism and masochism. In addition, I explore some of Fanon's notions, such as victimization and moralization.

The Other was reclothed, dressed in moral attire, then one wonders do I write through my body or does it write itself or do I have a body of my own or is it stolen from me.

This book acts as a fabrication to the voices I hear in the United States as a foreign worker, a professor teaching art history. The voices take me back to the scar of the British Empire, the in-between space; still, I love to be in the in-between space, to be the Other. The space allows me to capitalize on it, create a platform, a discourse, an aesthetics of postcolonialism. The in-between space though I often question and wonder do I have a choice . . . what with the voices that flutter around, ache against the skin, nevertheless today I will say it is a seductive space.

Me being a female body . . . these are a few lines I draw parallel between the colonized space and the female body's space between the legs and how similar it is to the in-between Space.

Between The Legs The Space[23]

The Space   Dis   pace

Dis/ease, Dis/favor, Dis/member, Dis/possess, Dis/rupt
Is that Space Evanescent, Transitory
NO
Its **VOLATILE**   though
The Space   Colonized
The Space   Sacrificed
The Space   Possessed
The Space   Raped
The Space   Disrupted
The Space   Victimized
Don't Forget   The Space used as Excessessssssssssssssss
The Tool for Male Pleasure
Forever to be Fucked
That Dirt won't   won't Wash away
Even scrubbed
The marks, memories linger onnnnnnnnnnnnnnnnnnnnnnnnnn
But I think
That **Space**   **Woman**   don't forget
The Erotic Power
It's **VOLATILE**   USE IT
To erupt, explode
To make Powers fly
And Occupy the Space
Bitch I tell you its very Explosive
You can be **Celebrated**   **Between the legs**   the Space

—*Rekha Menon*

Re-dress Cosmos

Dress Me Up by Rekha Menon. Published by Signet books in 2000. Cover art by Miss Menon known for the raw emotion she could pack into the cover. A perfect match for the story about a crime genius and an amoral wench. "They might have made it if it hadn't been for the dirty, stinking "INDIAN" coming from a downtrodden, poverty ridden country, with a stench riding on tigers and playing elephant polo, living in tree houses.........a perfume unberable...........and a certain seductive Indian tempting witchcraft ....never-theless SHE was a SEDUCTIVE INDIAN TEMPTRESS........called ???????. INDIAN PRINCES ....

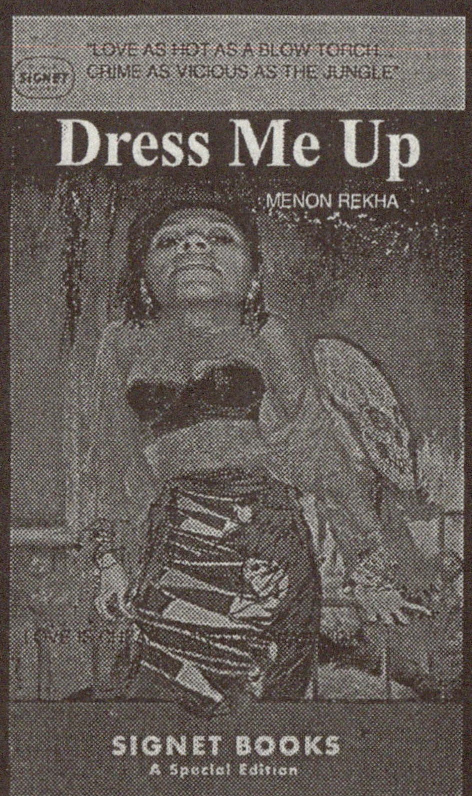

WHERE DO WE GO FROM HERE?   WHAT ABOUT TOMORROW?   WHAT ABOUT YESTERDAY?
READ THE BOOK...........DON'T MISS THE RAW EMOTION SPECIALLY OF 5th JULY
Its a great classic, cliched story you would never have read. The exotic, romantic, oriental story with under-lying text of KAMASUTRA playing a great role throughout the story. Kama, the sensuous, erotic love. Also don't miss the child-marriage, how she remembers her long lost child hero, and the great pompous ceremo-ny of 'SATI', (bride - burning). You will enjoy reading this EXOTIC ORIENTAL ADVENTURE.

1

Disrobing and Redressing

Excess of Judgments

The contemporary context, constitutive of various forms of judgments both of traditional and contemporary aesthetic works, shows that the major target of derision is both the expressive and the bodies stripped naked of expressivity, objectified or subjectified, that is, psychologized or moralized. What attracts such judgments is expressive excess, the cosmic, and yet what is judged is the "naked and immoral body?" I examine the ambivalence between attractive expressivity, the worldly dimensions that encompass, pervade, capture and move, and the stripping of such expressivity to constitute bodies for judgmental "observation." In this sense, we are made ashamed of our naked bodies, and yet, our bodies are paraded as inevitably expressive and thus "disturbing." This ambivalence leads the analysis toward the possibility of showing the contemporary "confusion" among Indian artists concerning the sense of their aesthetic creations.

Perhaps the confusion can be resolved, however, by showing that it is too late to resume the "purity" of traditional readings of the aesthetic; after all, we have gone through the colonial subjection that has become part of the contemporary context, and hence, our interpretations cannot bracket completely this context. It is too late to back up into history and start from some innocent point of inception. Although not directly cosmic, this participation is, nonetheless, a sharing of a common world that might provide an access to a reading of the cosmos that selects from both Indian and Western traditions. In this chapter, the interface of multiplicities of cultures, the re-reading of them will be discussed through the transgressions of the presence of the cosmic dance ritual and the aesthetics of art, yet the body politic of identity arises even if it is transgressed, disrobed and redressed.

West Casting a Shadow of Morals

With colonialism comes internalization of the passions, making them into personal emotions that have to be judged in terms of moral rules. This includes the judgment of bodies as engaged in individual sexual activities or even dancing that is morally prohibited as public display. This means that the erotic body which, in Indian tradition, captured the cosmic *kama*, is reduced to a body having sex, vulgar and judged, and therefore, immoral. The gaze shifts from the cosmic passion to the genderized bodies having sex. All these *kamic* excess forms and figures surely took on a major shift in interpretation with the entrance of colonialism. The forms and figures were pushed into the background and their visage became transformed in meaning. The forms shifted from the mythical-cosmic presence to becoming images of rational-empirical judgment. Where once the dynamism and the drives were, to a great extent, impersonal, now they tend to become personal. What once was comprised with a cosmic nexus and an overabundant force to achieve the *Brahman* as the trace of all pervasive cosmos, and the display of such arts which comprised *kamic* passions, explicitly depicting the cosmic union, was now questioned. The colonial period seems to me to have introduced the emotional response to art: the fear, disgust, anxiety, and, indeed, abstract feeling of approval and disapproval, of pleasure and or displeasure. The emotional reading of art/dance ritual shifted the gaze away from cosmic passions and their serene appreciation. The colonial period indeed brought in the question of morals, moralizing, gender, genderizing issues into art. It was not just colonialism, postcolonialism, but also neocolonialism.

Thus, the dimensions of Indian cosmic aesthetics/dance were judged not as revealing an area that transcends the characteristics of things while remaining worldly phenomena, but as characteristics of the things of the world. As Algis Mickunas would state, cosmic awareness is, in principle, different from all things, objects, subjects, and their collective characteristics. Such awareness is coextensive with the cosmos to the extent that it transcends all things, but does not transcend the world, does not regard the world from outside. It tracks the aesthetic dimensions that are directly lived prior to objectification and even psychologization; it is the domain of passive "engagement" that one lives through rather than conceives.[24] This cosmic awareness was completely missed and the aesthetic experience was marked by objectification and psychologization. In this context, Indian art/aesthetics/dance was reduced to things and judged by an excess of colonial moralizations.

The Transgression of Limitation of the Cosmic Presence

The traditional/classical dance rituals in the temple were transgressed and reduced to immoral *nautch*, dance equivalent to vulgar prostitutionalism. The temple rituals of *rangabhoga* and *angabhogha* necessitated the physical presence of women replacing the imaginative celestials, propitiating the gods as per the *agamic* prescriptions. The allegorical view of dance used for the purpose of the pleasure of the *devas*, and as a means of diverting the attention of the *rishis* from austeric practices, transformed into a divine service in the medieval temple traditions. As a result, temples vied with one another in having the best dancers and musicians in their services. Thus temple dancing was institutionalized and the dancing girls were patronized by kings and *mahajanas* and were often respectfully mentioned in many inscriptions of temples built in the medieval age. For example, an early Kannada inscription from Pattadakal of early Chalukyan times, 8th century A.D., reads: "Hail! The pillars of Challabbe, the harlot of the temple of Sri Vijayeshwara"—Challabe was the famous *Devadasi*, temple dancer who got the pillars made as votive offerings to God.[25] There are other inscriptions that portray dance as a respectful and a cosmic ritual, although performed by females. Some inscriptions record that dance was performed every evening when the community assembled for worship of the deity amidst the chanting of hymns. Rajaraja, the royal king, specially constructed two long streets just to house 400 dancers attached to the temple services.[26] These dancers represented the cosmically beautiful, sensuous celestial beings, like Rati and Rambha (Fig. 1.1), in beauty and the art of dancing. Hundreds of inscriptions

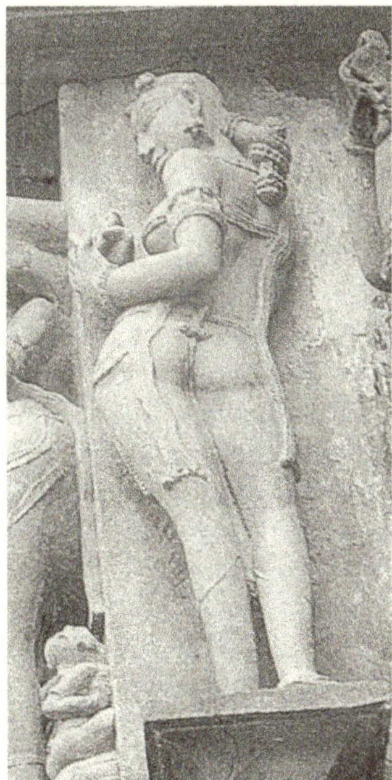

Figure 1.1. Celestial Dancer (like *Rati* or *Rambha*). Khajuraho Sculpture. Photograph by the author.

of this period use the word *Devadasi, Deva,* lord, *dasi,* friend and the temple activity was considered as a means of dedication.[27]

Slowly the *Devadasi* metaphor and the *Devadasi* system started losing its *bhakti,* tradition or essence, and was changing. The temples became a place of grandeur and celebration of events, and the dancing girls were more exhibition-istic in their presentation. The girls dedicated to temple services normally were unmarried and they acquired woman's power around the temple space. They even performed rituals like *rangabhoga* and they were respected and given the status of a *Swamini,* which originates from the word *Swami,* which means Lord, and the *Devadasis* were regarded as *Sani,* originating from *Swamini.*[28] This was definitely suppressed and disrupted by the verticality of the emerging patriarchal, hierarchized power. Later, due to factors like economic constraints, tantric practices, and free sex enjoyed by the *siddhas, jangamas, charanas,* patrons and priests and, not to forget, the colonial rulers with their hierarchical subjection of "the Other" and especially the "woman," these dancers were victimized to become public women and were completely equated with prostitutes.

The term *Devadasi,* which was used in the divine sense, was replaced by the term *Bhogastree,* and dance and music were used as a means of attracting clients. In colonial times, they were referred to as *nautch* girls, who were associ-ated with those "sisters of shame" and had to earn their living by arts other than dance, but who used this art of dance as an additional means of allurement.[29] With the degradation of the *nautch* came the degradation of the art, and the spiritual degradation was accompanied by the social. The dance that was held in respect was now immoral, disrespectful due to certain norms of prudery that were introduced to India by the alien/colonial rulers. The British government in India, in order to uplift and emancipate women, through education, and protect them from social evils, abolished the *Devadasi* system, as they have done with *Sati,* which they took for granted as imperfect, immoral and perverse.[30] As a result of this, the cosmic interpretation of dance was totally lost; in its place these dancers and the dance were reduced to *nautch* girls equivalent to prostitution. Because of the social stigma and change of status attached to these women, dancing in India came to be looked upon as a vain and vulgar pursuit, the lowest in the patriarchal hierarchy of things. The Indian dance, and thus woman as cosmic origin, was veiled with defamation.

Despite these difficulties and social abhorrence, there was a renaissance of Indian dance. This is due to the great reverence of the entire class of *Devadasis,* who were regarded as the repository of the tradition in most difficult situa-tions, from Vedic to colonial times. The present style of Indian dance finds its substance from the *Dasiattam* of colonial times, which definitely evolved into a rigid format. It nevertheless resuscitated all forms of Indian dance as whole, although rendered in very formal and rigid style; however, it did save the tradition from sinking into oblivion. The revival definitely changed the traditional concept of the cosmic, and the sensuality, sexuality, and spirituality, which were unified in one body of the dancer, were totally disregarded. The form became very orthodox, rigid with regulations of staging, and even changed from the temple space to a stage (see Fig. 1.2).

In time, the dance style and format evolved into different pathways. Although the dance was revived, the spiritual and cosmic aspect was lost in the modern age. The dance has been affected by cinema, technology, and a tendency to incorporate and ape dances and rhythms of the West in Indian films. One pathway provides decadence of the classical style and another provides the very rigid, classical form, the high art, which has an honored place in popular esteem and also has accompanied the emergence of Indian dance as an art with international status.

In contemporary India, there are a few dancers/choreographers such as Chandralekha, who are trying to revive the cosmic concept of dance. Her choreography is called *Raga: In Search of Femininity*. She says that this piece was created to summon the spiritual cosmic (Fig. 1.3). Her *Raga* aims to embody the unseen self that hovers in between, that is neither male nor female. Her work

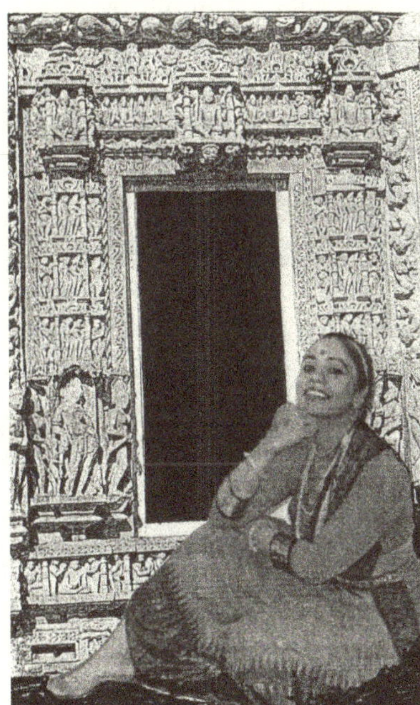

Figure 1.2. Dancer (author performing in front of the temple). Personal photograph.

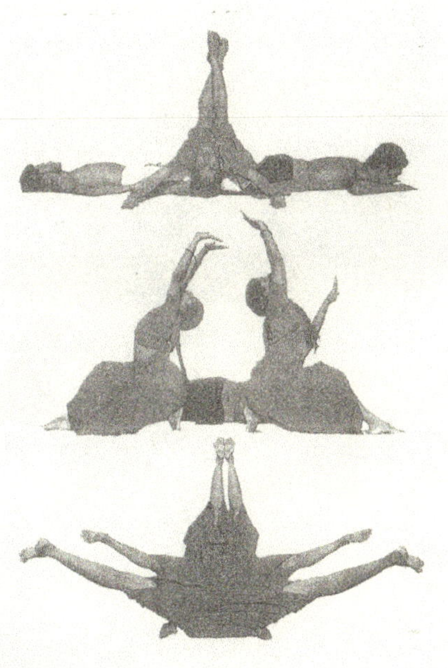

Figure 1.3. Chandralekha's Choreography— *Raga: In Search of Femininity*. Photograph courtesy Sadanand Menon.

was partly inspired by the 10th-century poet, Devara Dasimayya.[31] Dasimayya's poem captures the moment, the rhythm that is neither man nor woman, which Chandralekha tries to encapsule in her dance formations:

> If they see
> breasts and long hair coming
> they call it woman,
> if beards and whiskers
> they call it man:
> but look, the self that hovers
> in between
> is neither man nor woman.[32]

Chandralekha tries to revive the tradition of the cosmic as a rhythmic union. Thus, she abolishes fixed gender like the *Shivalingam*, because her compositions portray the cosmic union of the *lingam* and *yoni* (*lingam* as the phallic symbol and *yoni* as symbol of the female genitalia, portray the union, *Prakurti*, nature + *Purusa*, human, Divine + natural), just as all life does as participant in the cosmic union. This is achieved by embodiment and being passionate, where, as she says, sensuality, sexuality, and spirituality are all unified in the body. She says that her work is about linking inner and outer spaces.[33] She portrays the primal energy from the Tantric and early Vedic tradition and wants to refute the *Shivalingam* as sexual objects where the *lingam* and *yoni* are reduced to sexual organs rather than symbols of divine order. This, then, is where the self becomes impassioned in the passionate creation and expression of the dance and is merged in the cosmic rhythms.

Angika (Fig. 1.4) can be regarded as Chandralekha's manifesto of the cosmic body in dance. It presents the turbulent, yet joyous, evolution of dance through its origins in the cosmic energies where the warrior and animal move-

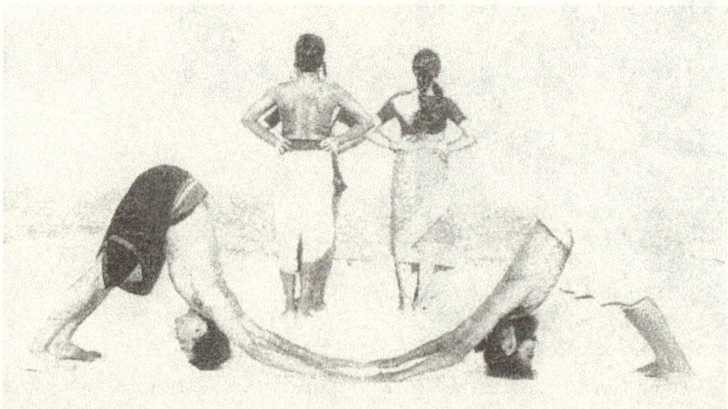

Figure 1.4. Chandralekha's Choreography—*Angika*. Photograph courtesy Sadanand Menon.

ments are crystallized in the primary movements of the dance radiating forth the cosmic energies. In the second half of this *Angika* composition, Chandralekha portrays the socialization of dance, taking from Bharata's concept of *Sharira mandala*. Our body is the center of the universe, yet this inspired body language changes across time, where the essence and content of the body got diverted, fragmented, and negated. First, the body became a vehicle of the gods, then a vehicle to serve kings, courtiers, men from *Devadasi* to *Rajadasi*, and then, the body became a victim of moralistic society and the dancer an object of social contempt.[34] This composition shows Chandralekha's attempt to revive the traditional dance as cosmic, but then, she is held back in her composition in order to show the present transgression of cosmic energies by the socializing, genderizing of dance and, in turn, the victimization of femininity and the female body. At the end of the composition, she does try to revive the cosmic energies by showing that *Angika* has to do with bodies and how they work to bring forth cosmic energies as significant to ourselves as worldly events.[35]

Her innovations are widely acclaimed internationally, although there has been a lot of controversy in India from traditional classical dancers who, I would say, misinterpret the cosmic tradition. The veteran critic Subudu, whose word goes a long way in promoting a dancer's career, begins his review of Chandralekha's performance, in the Delhi edition of *The Statesman*, by invoking the tale of the Emperor's new clothes, and concludes by echoing the child's words: "Mummy the Sultan is stark naked." Continuing in this ascerbic mode, the review accuses Chandralekha for assiduously trying to go back to the stone age on the pretext of harnessing primordial energy through dance forms. This was followed by the punchline: "One hopes she does not revert to raw meat."[36] This criticism reflects, in a way, the patriarchal stranglehold of dance in India today. Despite Chandralekha portraying the cosmic energies as a vital embodiment in dance, the latter is now critiqued, stripped, transgressed from its cosmic presence.

The dance and musical metaphors depict the cosmic maternal presence: This is in contrast to the rigid quadrature of patriarchy during colonialism. For the logic of this patriarchal system, dance was disruptive. This seems to me one of the reasons why the colonial systems were quite unhappy with the gyrating Shiva and the dancing girls, and hence, had to reduce them to prostitution. Eventually the cosmic, maternal presence had to be suppressed. This is what has happened in contemporary India, when Chandralekha's compositions are vehemently critiqued to suppress the cosmic maternal presence in dance.

Trendy Exoticism

The exotic transgression of the Indian dance ritual on the other hand is very popular, trendy and in vogue today in the West, esspecially with the diaspora artists, where ethinicity/identity/Indianness play a great role. One can see the merging of the global and local, the flows interfaced. This is where one can note the body politic of the colonized over the colonizer. For instance in New York City, Lata Mangeshkar's (Indian popular singer) songs are addictive, and are infused with the hip-hop beat. Her songs are monster hits on club floors and radio stations throughout the country. Very few of the people who are dancing to the song and mouthing its lyrics understand the words—not that it matters. All kinds of people love her song, remarks DJ Rekha—she frequently features the track at dance events. One sees the Bollywood image, just like the Hollywood image, is catching up—*Taal*, Indian beat in the background, this track kicks ass—in true Indian style, it is hotter than Vindaloo curry, says DJ Rekha. The use of Bollywood vocals is just a stroke of genius wrote a listener of the BBC; another said, it is simple, the beat kicks in and makes it danceable. Another example is the *Masala Bhangra* girl. Tanmaya Kumar Nanda notes in the article 'The Masala Bhangra Girl,' from *India Abroad*, dance fitness instructor, Sarina Jain (often referred to as the 'Indian Jane Fonda') conducts *bhangra* workouts at some New Yorks's top exercise clubs. *Bhangra* is a Punjabi folk dance form, which is used for the trendy beat. *Masala Bhangra* (Fig. 1.5) blends high-energy aerobic steps with *bhangra* dance steps, salsa, and hip-hop for a fun-filled vigorous cardiovascular workout accompanied with drum beats played on a *dhol* drum.[37] This has become so popular that the *bhangra* girl is invited to conduct courses in fitness centers and her videos have spread to the East and West coast. One can note in this example the trendy exotica, the touristy trend, the fad for exotica.

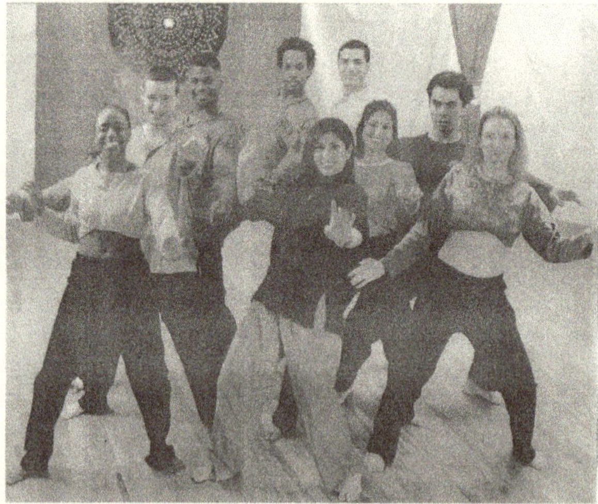

Figure 1.5. Masala Bhangra. Sarina Jain, fitness instructor in the center of the photograph. Photograph courtesy Sarina Jain.

Cosmic Eroticism Dressed in Moral Space

The traditional arts, the *Mithuna* sculptures (Figs. 1.6 and 1.7), were judged either as immoral with respect to the globalizing morality, or as uncreative with respect to other phases of the global logics of subjective inventiveness. In this sense, the traditional Indian aesthetics that were regarded as cosmic became regarded as subjective, interest-laden expressions, or social promotions of traditional Indian power holders. This subjectivation of the cosmic eroticism later was drawn into the globalizing process as exotic material to be sold for a price. The *Upanishad* texts and the various interpretations of what these *Mithuna* sculptures actually portrayed were taken out of context of the cosmic expressivity and were judged as immoral, pornographic, or touristically exotic.

Today, in the art scene in India, or for the immigrant artists in Western cities, all these forms, the *Mithuna* sculptures, the *kama* (love, desire) in excess, and figures, took on a major shift in interpretation with the entrance of colonialism/globalization. The forms shifted from the mythical-cosmic presence to becoming images of material, spatial bodies, with exposed organs. The pervasive cosmos, the display of *kamic* passions, explicitly depicting the cosmic union, was now questioned. The colonial period seems to me to have introduced the

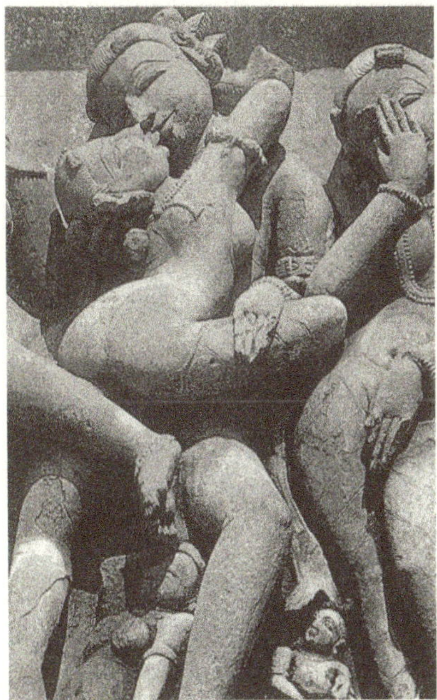

Figure 1.6. *Mithuna* sculpture. Khajuraho. Photograph by the author.

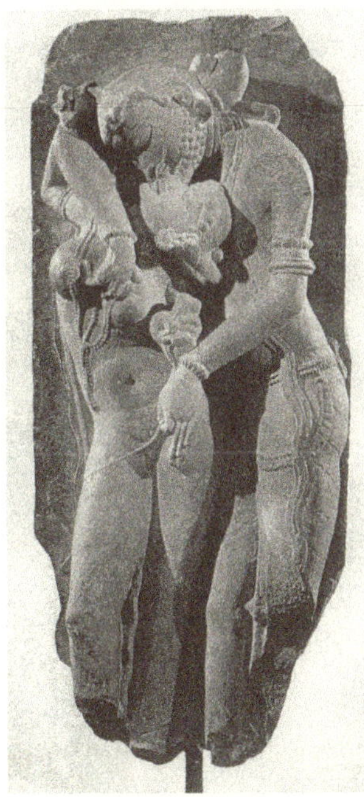

Figure 1.7. *Mithuna* sculpture. Khajuraho. Photograph by the author.

emotional response to art; the emotional reading of art shifted the gaze away from cosmic passions and their divine appreciation.

A few examples of the contemporary period show that the colonial period indeed brought the question of morals and moralizing, gender and genderizing issues into art: "The British even said the sculptures at Khajuraho were extremely indecent, obscene and offensive specially to find them in the temples that professed to be erected for good purposes on account of religion; everywhere there are a number of female figures who are represented dropping their clothes and thus purposely exposing their persons."[38] The British said the art was indecent and obscene, forgetting the cosmic nexus, union, and aesthetics of Hindu art. But they did colonize us and our art and how we perceive art today. They have inbred us to subjectify, genderize, and personalize art and limit us to things, objects, sex, biology, commodity. Although in the contemporary period artists have tried to move back to the cosmic *lila* play, nevertheless, even this thread has changed or, should I say, became colored and embedded with the prudish colonial impact, such that now we read the contemporary art through the British imperial attitude.

Kanayi Kunhiraman's sculpture, for example, the *Yakshi* (Figs. 1.8 and 1.9), evidences the colonial impact. *Yakshi* signified the mother goddess, fertility goddess, who from her nature brings forth its fruits. Yet, *Yakshi*, who is the force of creation, source of energy, the *Shakti*, the earth goddess, *Prithvi*, is completely looked down on, vehemently criticized: there were even protests against Kunhiraman's sculpture being publicly displayed. The intriguing question is: What happened to the symbolic signification of the cosmic expressivity, when the *Lajja Gauri*, fertility goddess, boon-giving sculpture was not questioned? Why, now, instead of being a maternal force, is this figure genderized, this form regarded as a female exposing herself? The *kama* that was depicted as

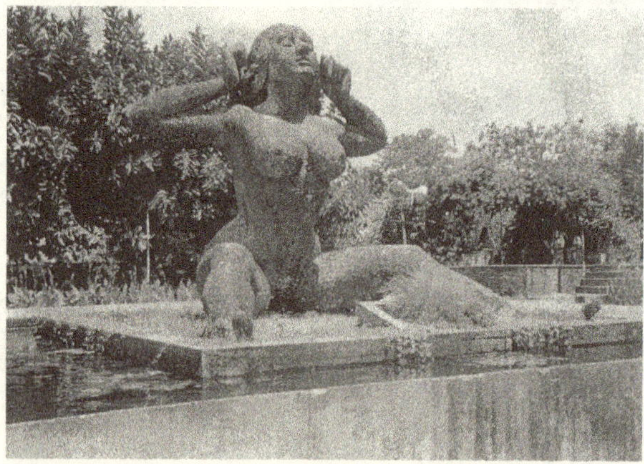

Figure 1.8. *Yakshi* (front view). Kanayi Kunhiraman's sculpture at the Malampuzha gardens. Photograph by the author.

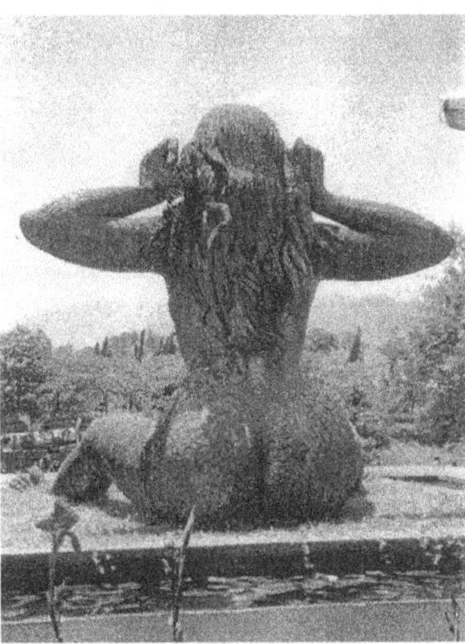

Figure 1.9. *Yakshi* (back view). Kanayi Kunhiraman's sculpture at the Malampuzha gardens. Photograph by the author.

the cosmic is gone; it is replaced by the objectified things and their oppressive relationship, in western fashion.

Paintings by M. F. Hussain also attract the fanatic political wing of India. Being a Muslim and a very famous popular painter who is celebrated by the media, he is inevitably placed in the midst of controversies. His execution of Hindu images provoke the ire of Hindu fundamentalists. An image drawn by Hussain portrays *Saraswati* (Fig. 1.10), the divine image, nude under water. The

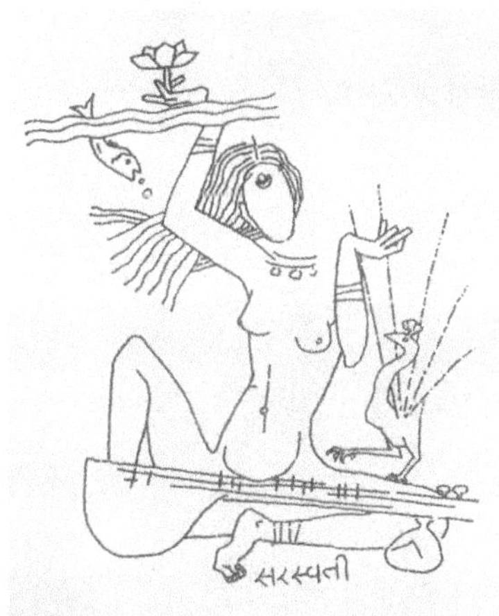

Figure 1.10. *Saraswati.* Drawing by M.F. Hussain. Courtesy Pundole Art Gallery.

controversies surrounding this image were galore. After all, she was portrayed nude and stripped of the moral code. Surprisingly the Hindu fanatics maintain that the divine images cannot be shown nude, because it is unethical and immoral. (Does this not ring a bell of the colonial times?) The uproar was unwarranted, because there was nothing sensuous or explicitly erotic in this figure, which was a sketchy figure of a nude female portrayed as *Saraswati*. The focus must be on the symbolic iconic elements added to it, and it was titled *Saraswati* written in Hindi script. The uproar had to do with Hussain being a Muslim who was portraying the Hindu religious images, according to the fanatics, in an improper manner. This example shows, ironically, how contemporary India still breeds the atmosphere of colonial morality. The staunch Hindus, who follow the colonial morality, claim it to be the Hindu doctrine and code. Why do these taboos abound? Have they forgotten the traditional cosmic glory of Khajuraho and Konark, which still loom large on the temple facades? The *kama* that was depicted as the cosmic is gone; it is replaced by the objectified things and their oppressive relationship, in Western fashion.

Looking at these changes stemming from the colonial period, one feels that the British absolutely played a great role in colonizing our Being. We have even lost great writings by women in India, although some are being retrieved now as fragments of these writings, for example, Muddupalani's poetry. An 18th-century Telugu poet, Muddupalani was a poet in the court of Pratapasinha, who reigned between 1739 and 1763. She wrote a great work called *Radhika Santwanam*, on her abundant cosmic desires. The epic work denotes the longing for her desires. She writes about Radha and Krishna, as she herself is Radha yearning for the cosmic desire. A verse from Muddupalani's erotic epic *Radhika Santwanam* (Appeasing Radhika), translated by B.V.L. Narayanarow, states:

> Move on her lips the tip of your tongue; do not scare by biting
>   hard.
> Place on her cheeks a gentle kiss; do not scratch her with your
>   sharp nails.
> Hold her nipple with your fingertips; do not scare her by
>   squeezing it tight.
> Make love gradually; do not scare her by being aggressive.
> I am a fool to tell you all these.
> When you meet her and wage your war of love
> would you care to recall my "do's and don'ts," Honey?

This erotic epic poem was first published in 1887, and a second edition with a commentary was brought out in 1907 by Venkatanarasu, a linguist.[39] Neither of the editions satisfied Bangalore Nagaratnama, a courtesan herself. She reprinted the work that she considered the proper translation and published it in

1911. Nagaratnama's edition was banned by the British, who regarded this text as corruptive of the minds of people.[40] Its "obscenity" and "indecency" would, according to the British, demoralize the good institutions. Muddupalani's work during the Tanjavur period of Telugu literature was acclaimed as a melodious great work and she as a great poet. But the very work was not only banned by the British, but also criticized by Kandukuri Veereshalingam, father of the social reform movement in Andhra and a novelist himself. He dismissed the poet and denounced her work in no uncertain terms. "This Mudddupalani is an adulteress," he wrote, "Many parts of the book are such that they should never be heard by a woman, let alone emerge from a woman's mouth. Using *Sringara rasa*, emotion, sentiment, as an excuse, she shamelessly fills her poems with crude descriptions of sex."[41] The poem, he concluded, was pernicious. Of course, he forgot the cosmic nature of the poetry and the cosmic desire. It was only in 1947, with the support of the nationalist leader Tanguturi Prakasam, that the ban orders were removed and permission granted to publish Nagaratnama's edition of *Radhika Santwanam*.[42] The new edition was published in 1952. But in the late 1980s, when the editors who published the fragments searched for a copy of her work, they had difficulty in finding it, and were assured by critics that her work was obscene and simply not worth reading, even though many of them had not even seen the text.

The book is no longer banned, but it had been decreed out of existence ideologically. Poets such as Muddupalani, who had been acceptable figures in royal courts, came to be regarded as debauched and their art as corrupting. The British thought that India was the White man's burden and had to be taught the ways of being moral and decent. One administrator from the British government reported that, "the natives must either be kept down by a sense of British power or they must willingly submit from conviction that the British are more wise, more just, more humane and more anxious to improve their condition than any other rulers they could have."[43] Another observed that Indian literatures contained neither the literary nor the scientific information required for the moral and mental cultivation so essential if good government was to be desired and appreciated.[44] Only suitable moral literary works, which have a fine-grained ethical sensibility, should be entrusted for the authority and moral codes of the British to be recognized. In Mayo's book, an explicit political agenda was mentioned where Mayo concludes that Indians were not ready to rule their own country because, among other things such as inferiority, ignorance, ineffectiveness, immorality, they overindulged in sex.[45] Thus, *Radhika Santwanam* was immoral, dangerous, and Muddupalani reprehensible and indecent, and her work marginalized and delegitimated. We are still living with these colonial morals: we judge art, poetry, aesthetics today by gender-izing, moralizing and psychologizing. No wonder that when they searched for Muddupalani's book in the 1980s, it was difficult to find a copy.

Contemporary eros has changed its tone from the cosmic to the psychological and subjective, which is the colonial imperial attitude. Yet, artists who interpret their work as a commitment to values, sensitive to the colonial interpretations and views, are beginning to appreciate the cosmic aesthetics of India and are trying to transgress the British, colonized limitations. As such efforts are, however, within the available modernity-tradition polarity framework, it is difficult to see these efforts in anything other than dichotomous terms. Ideologically speaking, one still presupposes totalitarianism, and thus, those who see from this polarized perspective can only approve of a change that is in consonance with modernity. The only destiny that is envisaged for tradition is that it, too, must be modernized.

This dichotomy exists not only today, it was there even when the British ruled India. Chiplunkar (1850–1882), a man of letters, who in 1874 started a journal called *Nibhandmala*, focused all discussion on the problem of the country. The journal's theme was "*Amachya Deshachi Sthiti*," "The State of our Country." The following were some observations, "Crushed by English poetry, our freedom has been destroyed . . ."; the rest of the sentence reads that under British laws we have become bankrupt.[46] Using the term *English poetry* as a shorthand or synecdoche, Chiplumkar denotes the entire range of western intellectual influences. Chiplunkar's formulation is penetrating; it shows how profoundly the British had succeeded in holding not only the physical territory of India but also the minds of those whom they ruled.[47] Thus, Chiplunkar himself in the same text, *Amachya Deshachi Sthiti*, considered it a "matter of good fortune" that without our doing "we are destined to come in contact with a country possessing such incredible efficacy." Among the advantages Chiplunkar listed the acquisition of a vast capital of knowledge:

> practical gains like the railways, the post and telegraph; and the coming in of law and order. . . . 'How lucky we are,' this vast body of knowledge from the West has just walked over into our land on its own . . . the infusion among Indians of commendable new traits, such as desire for independence, national pride in one's self, a revulsion against improper conduct . . . is essential for the country's advancement, without this new knowledge the country would remain backward, as English education advancing in this country I predict progress, independence and happiness.[48]

I should say that Chiplunkar's prediction is the same as the globalizing logic, the instrumental rationality in the guise of a postcolonial author. In short, the colonial body is embodied into the British modern period as a form of "naturalness." One becomes healthy and wise; here one becomes a part in a metonymic circulation of images and functions.

The global images are so obvious in the global advertising campaigns. The ads contribute to the belief that success and beauty are brand names with a distinctly White American look to them. Trade journals *Advertising Age* and *Business Abroad* note the trend: "World-Wide Beauty Hints: How Clairol Markets Glamour in Any Language."[49] This brief statement is purely metonymic. Clairol does not present us with images for our "mental" contemplation, but "markets glamour":

> The advertising agency Saatchi and Saatchi is enthusiastic about "world branding" and global culture: Market research will be conducted to look for similarities not seek out differences. Similarities will be exploited positively and efficiently . . . developing advertising for an entire region of the world, and not simply for one market to find a real advertising idea so deep in its appeal that it can transcend national borders previously thought inviolate.[50]
>
> Western and Indian corporations are not alone in pursuing this ideal. Shiseido, the Japanese giant in cosmetics, has recently revamped its advertising to present a "determinedly international thrust." "It is easy to create an ordinary nice picture with nice model and a nice presentation for the product," explains a company executive, "but we wanted to be memorable without being too realistic, realism would have too closely defined our market." Shiseido hints at its Asian origin—"intrigue from the Orient"—but its models are white and its targeted market is "the international affluent elite." Saatchi and Saatchi agree that this is the strategy of the future.[51]

And to join the future one has to play the strategy, "join the club," you've got to look like this, smell like this, speak like this, and dress like this. This is the model of success and glamour, the vision of beauty that is familiar around the world. It is safe to say that we, Indians, benefit from a collective global fantasy of success and beauty defined by White skin, Western culture and imported products. There seems to be great desire to aspire to Western values and Western culture. Often an advertisement will be written in English because that is one way of flattering an audience: "You are smart, sophisticated and educated." I suppose that is why the models tend to be White. Indian television commercials are paean to the American way of life, full of glamorous movie stars and famous sports heroes. Despite a growing pride in things in our own country, the United States remains a cultural pacesetter for India. If an advertising company does not find an American celebrity to endorse its product, the company may opt for displaying the product in a recognizably U.S. setting or placing a blue-eyed, blonde model alongside of it. An example of a fashion show portrays this White Western model as the more sophisticated and more beautiful, or is this an Indian model with the Western look and comportment

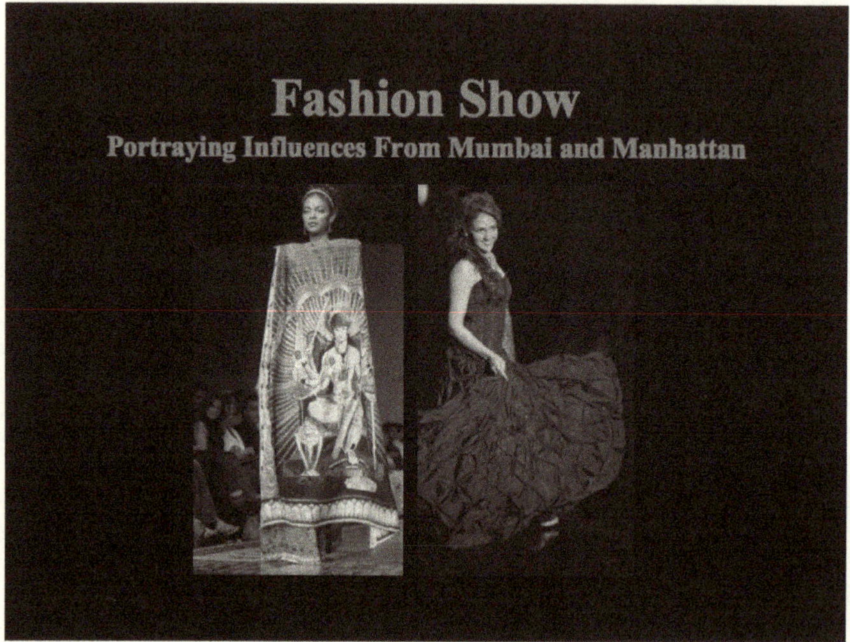

Figure 1.11. Fashion Show (portraying influences from Mumbai and Manhattan). Personal photograph.

(Fig. 1.11). Its not just the fashion industry or in beauty, but Indian space, the Third space, is also catching up in the aspect of the living space. Don't miss a Florida Paradise in India (many replicas like this peaceful luxurious village in Florida are built in the outskirts of Bangalore and Hyderabad in India)—you can buy it, it is peaceful, it is a retreat nestling in the hills, its got everything, a club house with swimming pool, a Jacuzzi, gymnasiums catering to health consciousness . . . and outside the Santosh village, the Florida Paradise bank opposite the slums of India. India is surely catching up? . . . (Fig. 1.12). And, of course, India has cybercafes. These cybergiants of India, today the sultans of cyberspace (Fig. 1.13), do not allow one to miss their clothing, suited booted, these sultans of cyberspace, they believe in their life as Indian, but their vision is entirely to promote a globalizing logic.

This trend toward global cultural homogenization has not gone unchallenged. Indigenous culture remains a powerful alternative to the White Western model of success and beauty. Especially in India, and for Indians in Western cities, traditional images are officially promoted as a response to the flood of imported Western culture as part of a decolonizing process, or for national Indian identity. Sometimes local culture acts subversively as a bearer of otherwise

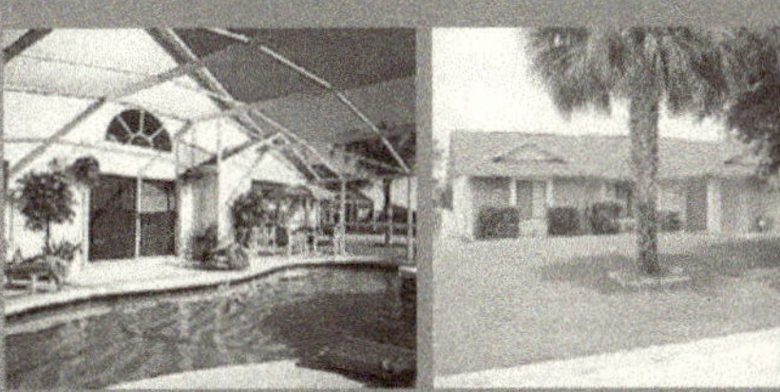

Figure 1.12. Santosh Village (Florida Paradise). Personal photograph.

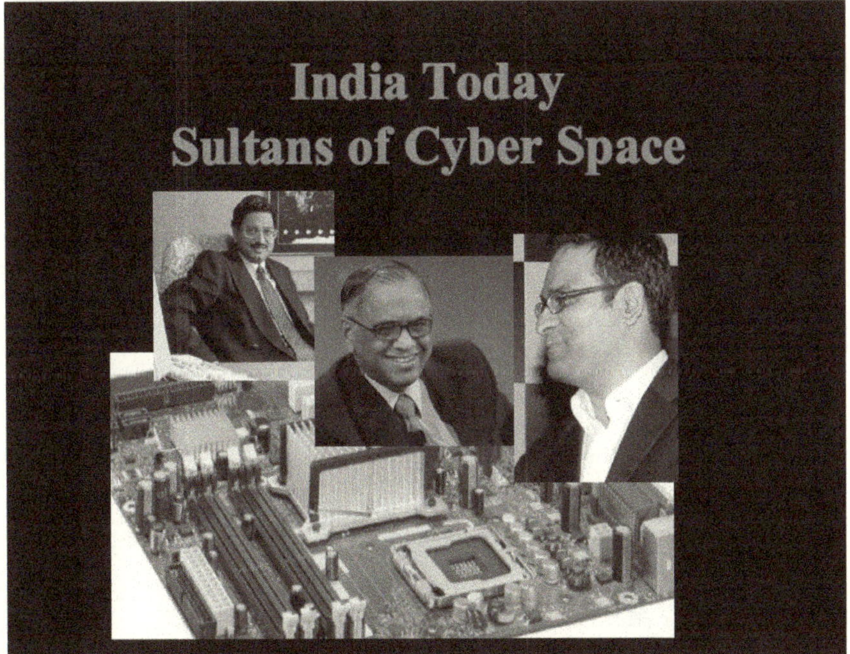

Figure 1.13. Sultans of Cyber Space. Personal photograph.

illegal messages of political, economic, and cultural resistance. It is interesting to note that it is women who are the bearers to reclaim, and in some cases to reinvent, the indigenous culture. Significantly, it is the women throughout the world who tend to be designated as the culture-bearers and given the burdensome responsibility of preserving traditional values and aesthetics. A great salable advertisement in this context in India is a matrimonial column where the ads for brides read: "High caste, Gujarati Hindu handsome boy, English-speaking, green card, well settled in U.S., with Western values invites matrimonial proposals from slim, fair, traditional Indian, Hindu, Brahmin girls, who adhere to traditional Indian values and customs."

In terms of historical and spatial aspects, this oleograph (Fig. 1.14) contrasts tradition with modernity. In this print, the spatial juxtapositions depict the popular movie heroine Hema Malini with a bicycle. The landscape portrays the opposition between an Indian foreground and a foreign horizon. The heroine is represented in a traditional manner, clad in sari with bindi and bangles; she assumes a sedate posture and respectability, while in the distance, in the opposite direction, she faces a new woman clad in Western clothes with a posture of her hand on her hip astride a scooter. This is an inappropriate mount for a woman of propriety. There is a disjunction between traditional foreground and modern distance; "the juxtaposition also suggests the complimentary technological narrative of past harmony and future industrialization, connoting the destructive, threatening modernity/globalization."[52]

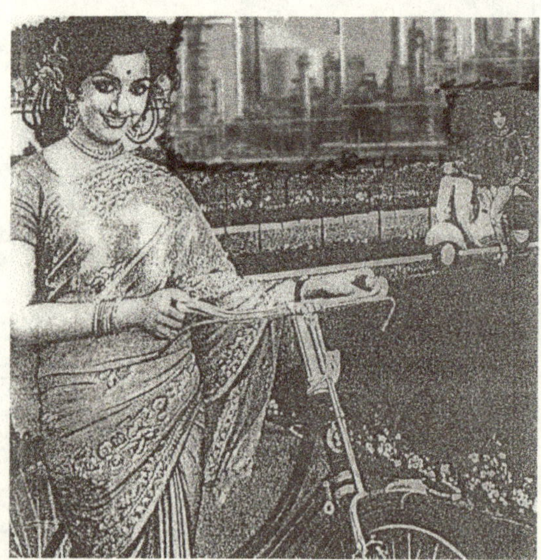

Figure 1.14. Oleograph. Calender print with actress Hema Malini (modified by the author).

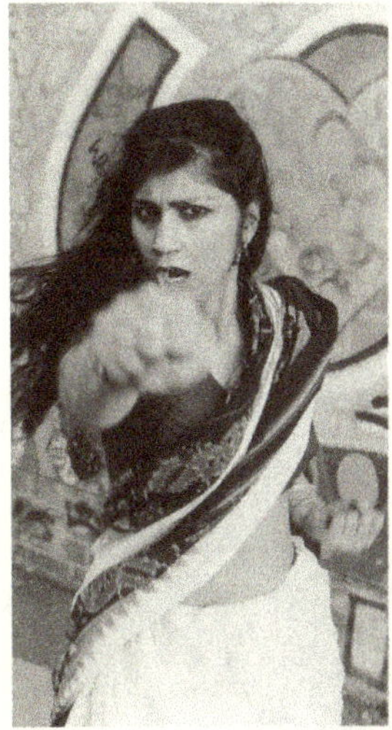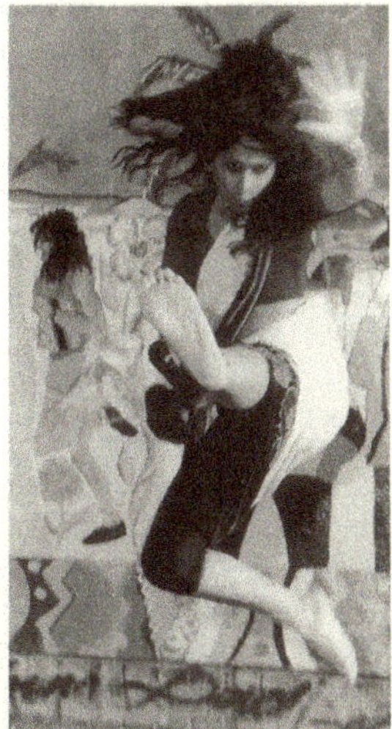

Figure 1.15. Burman's Auto-portrait (Chila Kumari Burman, in a sari performing the Japanese martial art of Shotokan, 1993). Photograph courtesy Chila Kumari Burman.

For example, let's discuss the contemporary artist Chila Kumari Burman who resides in London. Her work portrays the goddess Kali (Fig. 1.15) as one of the dominant representations which celebrates the dynamism, reclaiming empowerment and self-definition of the maternal in woman's image. On the one hand, she uses the Kali image as a self-definition of identity as an Asian woman, and on the other, to challenge the dominant Western stereotype of Asian femininity. She is reclaiming the image of an Asian woman in order to resist the racist stereotype of the passive exotic Asian. Through Kali, she focuses on affirmation of the female body as a symbol of resistance and self-determination. She uses the body as a weapon, in the image of the dark Kali, and shows a dominant image of the dark body as the racial Other who is inscribed as the locus of danger, desire, fear, and fascination.[53] Burman declares that her work, her self-portraits (Fig. 1.16) construct a femininity that resists the passive exotic Asian woman, imprisoned by male patriarchal culture. "Rather, I become the maker and definer of my own image, allowing me to challenge the viewers' preconceptions of Asian femininity."[54] The body prints, the self-display images are made by the artist covering her body with acrylics or Indian ink and then pressing it against a blank sheet of paper. These images insist a display of her identity; a declaration of an Asian woman artist working in Britain; it is also a snipe at the European tradition of the female nude.[55] Another example of her work (Fig. 1.17), holding different passports—Indian, Britain—the identity which portrays who you are. Who are YOU? This reminds me of my passport,

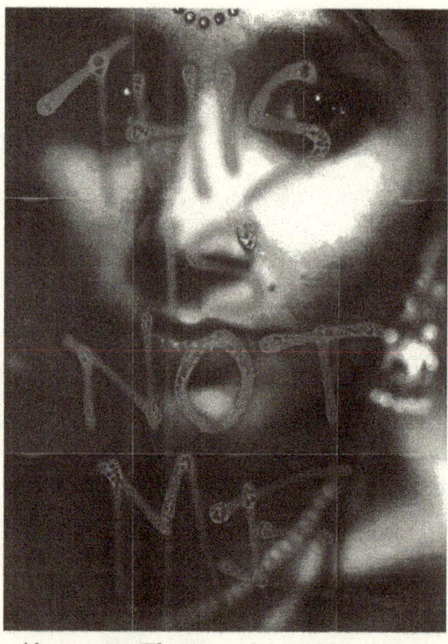

Figure 1.16. Burman's self portrait. *This is not Me, 1992.* Laser print and car spray paint. Courtesy Chila Kumari Burman.

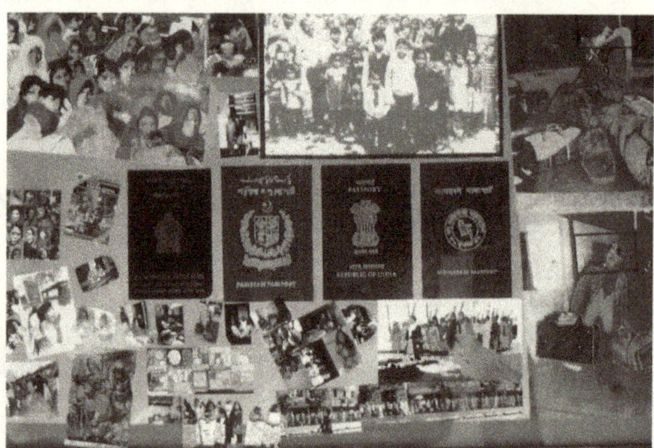

Figure 1.17. Chila Kumari Burman. *Convenience Not Love, 1986–87.* Color silkscreen and laser print. Courtesy Chila Kumari Burman.

my identity, the assumption of the immigration officer when I re-enter the United States, I can read him . . . "Do you speak English? Do you understand?" The stereotyping is so pronounced that it is hard to conceal.

Born in England, raised in India, and currently residing in the United States, Annu Palakunnathu Matthew has struggled with issues of identity and her relationship to the culture of her ancestry, her place of birth and her current place of residence. Her work, *Bollywood Satirized* and *An Indian from India* pose the question "Where do I belong?" She writes that her works are interpretations rather than a documentation of her life as an Asian-Indian woman living in a diaspora. In *Bollywood Satrized* (Figs. 1.18 and 1.19), Matthew brings out,

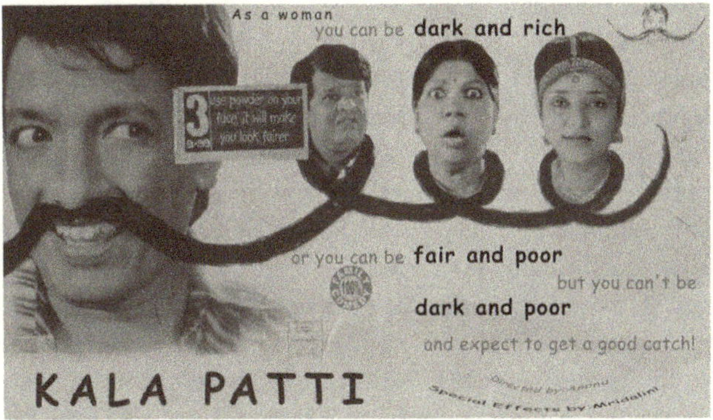

Figure 1.18. Annu Palakunnathu Matthew. *Bollywood Satrized, 1998–2000*. Inkjet print. Courtesy Annu Palakunnathu Matthew.

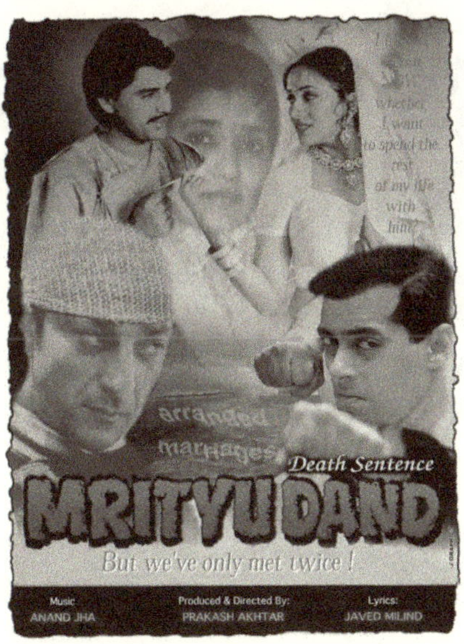

Figure 1.19. Annu Palakunnathu Matthew. *Bollywood Satrized, 1998–2001*. Inkjet print. Courtesy Annu Palakunnathu Matthew.

questions issues such as arranged marriages, the dowry system, discrimination based on skin color, attitudes toward "liberated woman," where she herself in the midst of this Indian milieu would be an alien. Although in Indian commercial movies, Bollywood portrays females as modern liberated women, the juxtaposition often is paradoxical. The movies' message as a whole, the moral that one takes home is often like the oleograph (see Fig. 1.14) that I have mentioned—she is modern, Westernized, she is no good, has no tradition, no culture. The proper shaping of a woman's place is preserving the traditional values, the docile, pure, fair, *Sita-Savitri*. In her work, Matthew portrays herself and shows the disjunction between tradition and modernity and how she/me are cast as an alien (not just here in the United States, but also back home in India too) for being liberated and Western-educated. Her other series of work, *An Indian from India* (Figs. 1.20, 1.21, and 1.22), poses questions often asked of her like where she is "really from" and often she has to clarify her origins as an "Indian from India," even though this description does not accurately characterize her relationship to India, England, or America.[56]

Matthew uses photographs "as a means of making connections to her own cultural background but also as a method of pointing out those aspects that distance her from the same heritage."[57] In these examples Matthew places herself alongside the American Indian—*On entry to the United States, 9 years later in Providence, Noble Savage/Savage Noble, American Indian with dot on face*

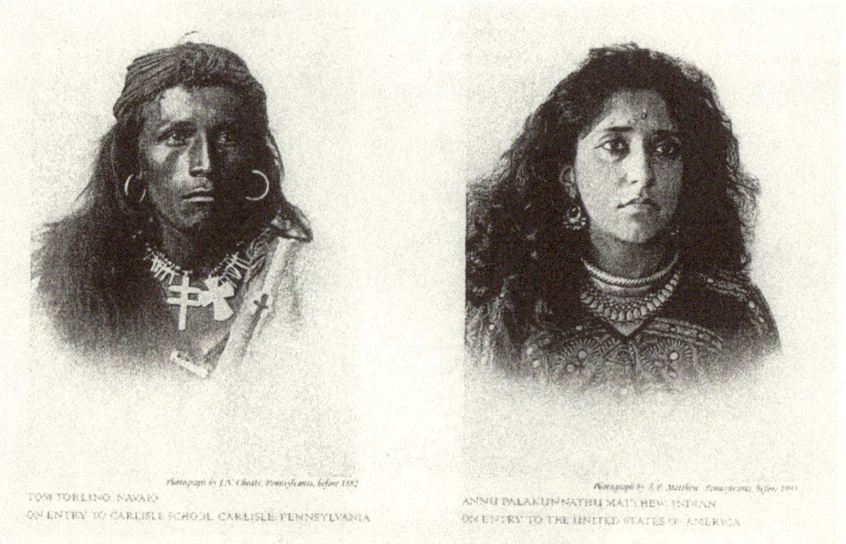

Figure 1.20. Annu Palakunnathu Matthew. *An Indian from India, 2001*. Inkjet print on watercolor paper. Courtesy Annu Palakunnathu Matthew.

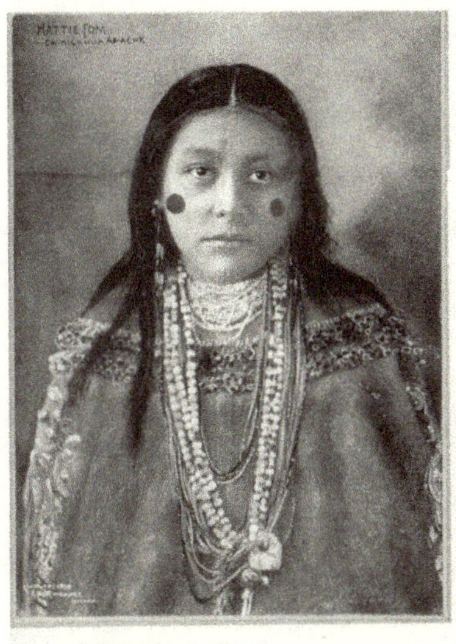

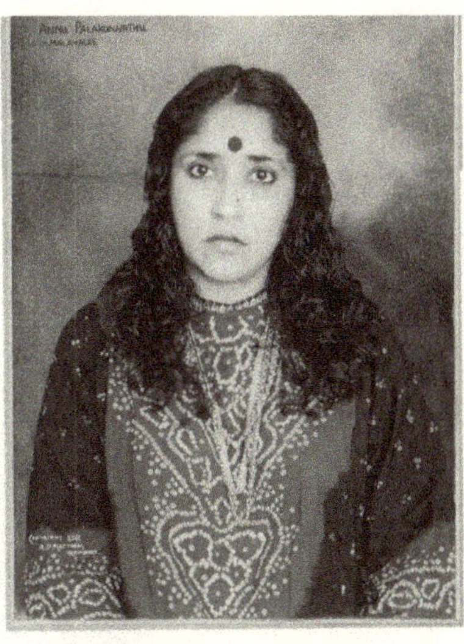

Figure 1.21. Annu Palakunnathu Matthew. *An Indian from India, 2001.* Inkjet print on watercolor paper. Courtesy Annu Palakunnathu Matthew.

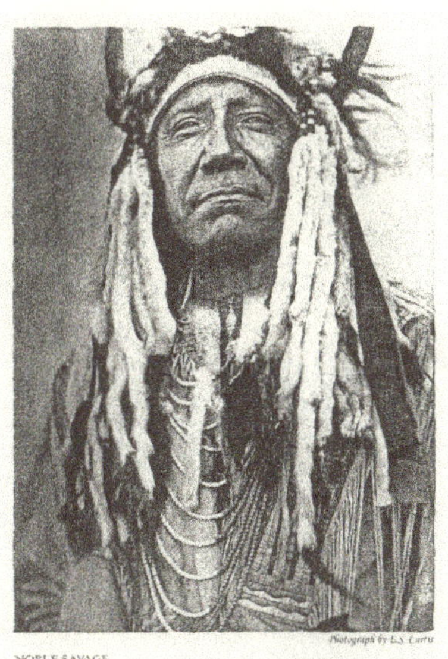

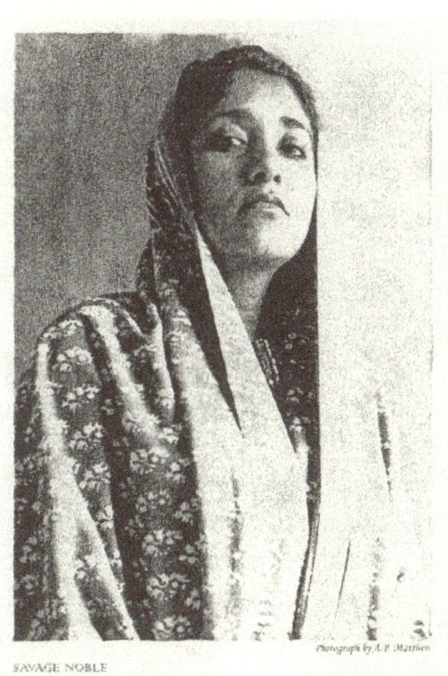

Figure 1.22. Annu Palakunnathu Matthew. *An Indian from India, 2001.* Inkjet print on watercolor paper. Courtesy Annu Palakunnathu Matthew.

and Indian American with dot on face—Matthew not only brings out the question of her origin, but also portrays the fascination of the West for the exotica, for the native clothing. The way the photographs are posed, expressed, she captures the Westerners' indulgence in the wealth of detailed material, the primitive, exotic, savage native look, just like the Victorian indulgence from the illustrated press to the encyclopedias of typical pictures of Indian natives.

A classic example of dressed in moral space, transgression of tradition in a different hermeneutic is the film *Fire*, written and directed by the Canada-based Indian immigrant Deepa Mehta. The film generated such uproar and instances of violence that officials finally prevented the film from running in India. *Fire* documents and explores tradition, social norms, taboos, through an ordinary setting of married, middle-class, conjugal family life. The film speculates on hypocrisies, tensions, and inadequacies, which are present in a patriarchal, heterosexual society. The film addresses the discordant arrangements of the two married woman, Radha and Sita, who apparently comply and cope with the family obligations, duty, so to speak. Radha had apparently coped with the exigencies of her situation. Her husband is attempting to free himself from "immoral" desires and thus, rejects erotic encounter. Yet, he insists that she be there for him to test his resolve. Of course, she is, according to her own *kamik* (love, desire) tradition, the very presence of desire; if the latter is abolished, then all, including her, are dead. She wants to bring *kama* back to life, irrespective of gender.

The newly wed younger woman, Sita, is far less patient. In this setting the intimacy between the two women burgeons and blossoms into an erotic-sexual relationship. This was the setting that was questioned, for the film was cast by viewers as a lesbian film and attracted Hindu fundamentalists of the right political wing, despite the director's disavowal. In an interview, Mehta suggests that this film is about choices not about immanent lesbian identities.[58] Nevertheless, the film was interpreted as a lesbian film. This theme, lesbian sexuality, was an unspeakable issue in contemporary India and thus created the uproar.

The power and terrorism of Hindu fundamentalists sparked such violent incidents, for instance, the burning down of the theater where the film was running, that the film was finally banned in India.[59] The film, for the Hindu fundamentalists, was improper, immoral, indecent, according to their reading of the Hindu norms of tradition. The fundamentalists' reactions and opinions they were airing were, "Is this what we are teaching our children? Let Shabana Azmi, who played the role of Radha, walk naked on the streets, no? How dare she enter our drawing rooms, making love to her own sister-in-law?"[60] Isn't it ironic of which tradition are they speaking? Have they not seen such blossoming cosmic *kama* on the Khajuraho walls? In fact, marking it as Lesbianism assumes Western sexual norms. Why is it that they do not read the film the other way, in terms of the cosmic *kama*, and not the British morality? Mehta actually interprets *Fire* as a test of women's resilience; she interprets this as a resistance and fight for life through mutual desire.[61] What is of crucial significance concerning the fire metaphor is the notion that woman, as the cosmic dynamism from *shakti* through *kama*, to Kali, is not reducible to gender: as Draupadi in *Mahabharata* is depicted, she is born of her own fire. This is to say that she is the very fire that cannot consume her. In this sense, the image of Radha cast into flames also states that she is the very flame that could not be extinguished. At one point, when Radha says that life is not worth living without desire, she crystallizes the premise of the film. One can even go back to the myth of *kama*, where without *kama* even Shiva would vanish; and I would say that this is our tradition.

The film also frames other perversions and norms of tradition by modernity. This perversion of today's India is contested relentlessly. In the film, Radha's husband, Ashok, is preoccupied with "religion" and wants to test his sexual control, reminiscent of Gandhi. He asks his wife, Radha, to lie next to him to see if he can control his temptation. According to Ashok's traditional norm, a proper Hindu can only have sex for procreation. Radha's physical inability to bear children gives him an excuse to abstain from sex and control his sexual urges. Is this a Hindu abstention, or is it a moralization that is couched in "religious" language. After all, if the husband needs "testing," he too reveals the inescapable *kamic* desire, just as was the case with Shiva. At least Shiva, as a proper representative of this tradition, was made to yield to this desire and continue the life of an entire cosmos. In this sense, a mere human, claiming to be "moral" and, hence, capable of escaping the cosmic *kama*, is completely foolish. If Shiva could not, how could Ashok? This really portrays what hermeneutic contortions a tradition is made to undergo and how they become the norm. Even the great Mahatma Gandhi was no exception. It is interesting to note how and what is considered proper according to tradition today; the power of suppression is all pervasive, but the Other, the suppresser, even in its denial, creates a tension that is between both.

In the interior north of India, a program called *Ghar-Vapasi*, returning home has been designed to reconvert Christians to Hindus.[62] The converted Christians were *Adivasis*, untouchables, who, during the British rule, had converted to Christianity. The missionaries sheltered them from the atrocities meted out on them by the upper cast Hindus, when the cast system became very prominent during the later Brahmanical crede and British rule. The *Adivasis* were outcasts and the upper strata of Hindus would not even touch them. Although these people found solace among the missionaries, one cannot forget that this was a strategy played out by the British to spread their rule and imperial power, as well as to condemn the Hindu "religion," so to speak. This program today is being conducted as another political campaign. The fundamentalist Hindus who belong to the conservative political wing, proclaim that India is a Hindu state and that today Hindus are a minority: Christianity has the whole world; all we want is to reclaim our Hindu identity, and our Hindu country. Thus, they want Christians in India today to reconvert to their original faith. And the politician, who is running for election, runs and uses this program on the pretext to welcome the *Adivasi*. Of course, initially he would not have touched them. Yet now one sees him washing their feet as a rhetorical image of welcoming them. He also says that they were converted forcefully by the British who used different allurements to convert them. What is relevant for my work is this: Hinduism, not being a religion, is, in fact, part of the Western vocabulary that the Hindu fundamentalists accept. In this sense, they are within the context of the bifurcated consciousness that is revealed in their anger and their wish to "convert" Others to their "faith."

It is to be noted that in Hindu tradition, no *guru* runs around in an effort to "convert" anyone to anything. Thus the fundamentalists act like Christians, while denying the West. The untouchables were the in-between group that was violated by both sides. No question that if they are true Hindus, their *karma* would allow them to be members of any so-called faith. My point is that the very secular political institutions of India are subverted by Hindu traditionalists who are completely imbued with British colonial attitudes.

Who Are We?

"Reflective" globalization, that is, various people reflecting about the globalizing processes, is creating the question of "who we are" among various ethnic, linguistic, regional groups, and even among individuals within such groups. Without either an imposition to which one may become resistant, or different from Others, questions of identity might not arise. Indians among Indians do not need to raise the question "Who are we?" A further aspect of the question of identity in contemporary art/aesthetics, or more generally, consists of the positioning of a group or individuals within a hierarchy: the colonial is "superior" and he makes us "inferior," thus forcing a reflection on ourselves and what makes us not only different, but even what, in our culture and ourselves, is "superior." The selective comparisons of oneself to the Other become a matter of defining one's identity.

How is the term *identity* to be understood in terms of personal, cultural, global contexts, and different spaces? Personal identity is not a given, but is maintained, repeated, and presumed to be continuous as a set of habitual activities or required responsibilities toward Others, hence, making the individual a core of normative (ethical) judgments: What you did yesterday will be still assigned to you today as your responsibility. You cannot say that the "self" that killed the Other person yesterday is not the same "self" who is now writing a book. The excuse in such cases is only if you were "insane" or someone forced you to do something. At the same time, one's personal identity arises only in correlation to and differentiation from Others. This is possible in a culture within whose parameters the individual assumes "useful" functions: one is an engineer, a farmer, a worker, a soldier, and hence one becomes a part in a network of socially defined functions-spaces, such as where and when one must be to perform such functions. But when one enters a globalizing trend, one is not only defined within one's own social-cultural parameters, one also obtains other identities and spaces-times. An engineer in India may be invited to perform tasks in Europe, or a defending soldier of Britain may be sent to insure the colonial rule. In these cases, what occurs is a compacting of identities: I am an Indian, Hindu, from a farming village, who acquired an education and is now working for Union Carbide in New York; hence I am also an immigrant, New Yorker, who has joined a Hindu temple to find a bride. In this sense, one may still be a citizen of India, but one is also looking toward becoming a citizen of another country. Thus, one is a knot of threads in a tapestry.

How is identity manifested in these different diasporas, spaces, cultures, and so on? In diaspora, either the immigrants or the refugees are confronting the Other world that may be quite alien to them, and this confrontation immediately reflects on their identity. They know that they are also Others, and, perhaps throughout their entire lives, will maintain their home identity more fervently than the persons who have stayed at home.[63] This is to say, their knowing their identity might be sharpened and more focused, maintained to a greater degree and hence more conservative. Of course, this kind of identity must take into consideration social classes and to what aspects of the new country such classes relate. Hence, the well-to-do immigrants from India, for example, will come to the West for even greater economic purposes, but they will also proclaim that they could never be cultural Westerners, because Western culture is vulgar-materialistic. In this sense, any solid research must be careful to address such social-class differences of the immigrants and the refugees.

The principle of identity is difference, that is, to recognize yourself requires the mutual recognition of the Other as different, and vice versa. The issue for globalization processes is not so much how to understand identity, such as individual identity in contrast to other individuals, or a group identity in the face of another group, ethnic, religious, even from village to village, or along family lines, but how is it that there are times during which the focus on this issue is pronounced? With globalizing wherein there is a promise to make us all "one humanity," "one global market," "the global village," and so forth, there is also a threat to make each group disappear into the anonymity of nondifferentiated mass culture. Thus, the Hindus seek to establish their sacred spaces (burn down the mosque), the Jews and the Muslims do the same in the face of "Western Satan," and the French are passing laws against "international" terms (meaning American slang), and the like. In this sense, there are various, numerous, faces of searching for and maintaining these newly "discovered identities," even if they are usually associated with some past event, or invented spaces. Because of the globalizing mobilities of people and the rearticulation of spaces, and thus, where one is and who one is, there appear multi-identities among individuals, ethnic groups, nations, and organizations.

I have shown one aspect of this interface of multiplicities of cultures. For me, the exercise has been a journey that suggests a context wherein my own aesthetic work can find a space-time as a conjunction of the "humanistic-expressive" and the "cosmic-inspiring." Yet, the journey is also a hope to continuously open and release us from the limitations that both metaphysics and ontology, of contemporary East and West, impose on us. To speak with one of the Western latecomers, would it not be wonderful to dance with the chances of the universe, and to laugh like no human has laughed before—with the cosmic laugh?

Inscriptive Seduction

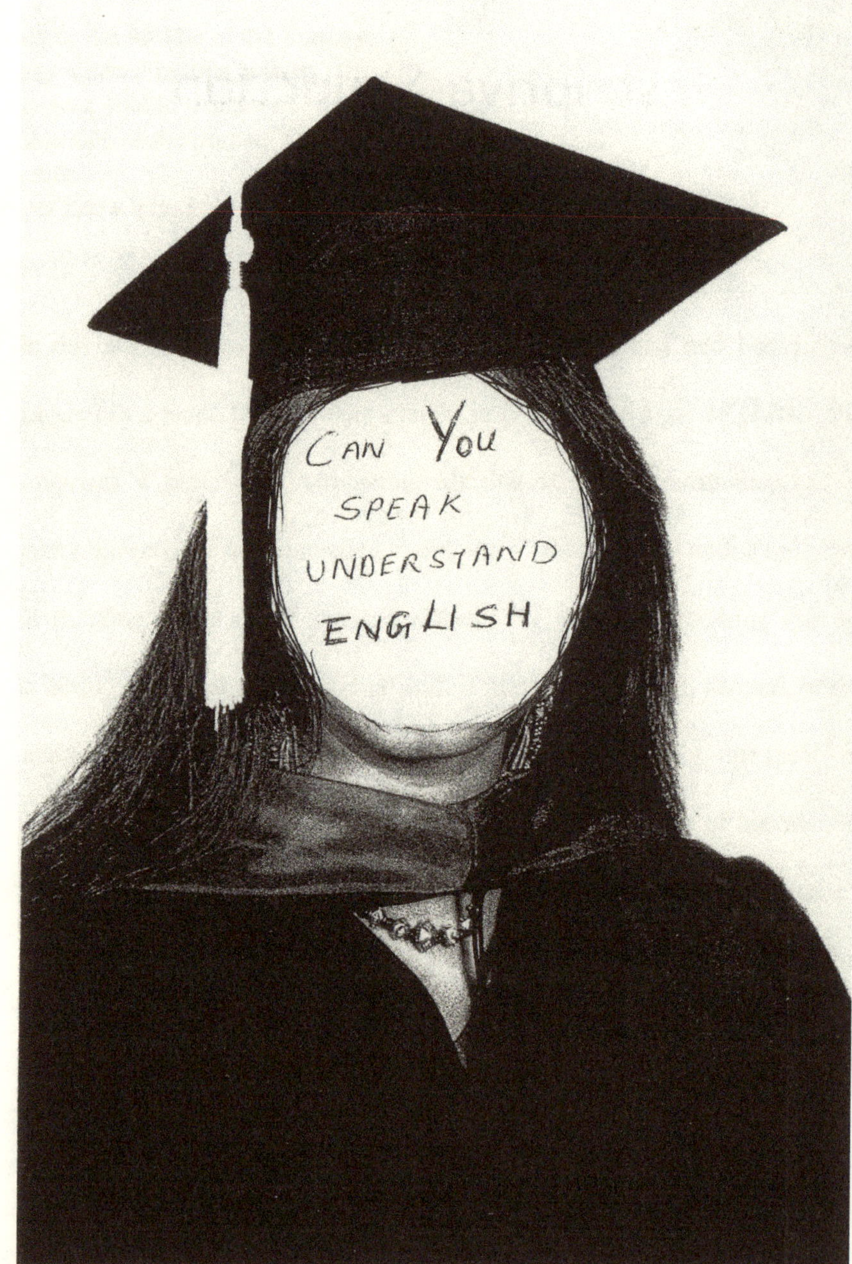

CAN YOU
SPEAK
UNDERSTAND
ENGLISH

2

Transgressions

Redressing Tradition

I am stuck in the middle of the journey
A highway without human activity
A text without visible structure
Life on this side of the border
On your side. . . .
I no longer know who I am but I like it

—"The Border Is . . . (A Manifesto)"[64]

In our postcolonial context, translation is interpretation and becomes a site, a space that creates a mode of self-interpretation in favor of the logic of globalization. The latter comprises a process of abolishing all that is local, traditional, and imposes homogeneity. Indeed, we are compelled to acquire a new subject—with a uniform, global look and thinking, in place of our old selves. The new is something that we must construct bodily on top of our traditional self: it must be exercised, painted, behaviorally proper, and uniformly predictable. All other forms of being a subject—the local—are to be relegated to the bin of primitivism, exoticism, inadequacy, and out of historical flow. In this context, this chapter investigates the contemporary Other/Otherness, some aspects of Indian art which was termed as primitive by the West, located in the local-historical Space, the immigrant Space, a local-Global India attempting to catch up with the Western Space. After all, the third world, me being from the third world, must catch up to the "world history" because our history is not part of the world. We are the Third Space, the Third World; we are attempting to be global and yet compelled to be local third. We are compelled to become subjects and objects of technical power and prowess, and yet we still cling to our traditional self.

41

Nevertheless this catching up, stripping and reclothing, redressing constitutes a double transgression: first, the colonial requirements transgress all bodily practices and expressive gestures and attires; second, the very imposition of the "proper" is transgressed by the indigenous bodies who are deemed "immoral but exotic and alluring" to be gazed at with eyes of desire. Given this context, the contemporary Other, Indian art/artists are struggling with both transgressions by attempting to strip the colonial moral garb from Indian bodies without at times succeeding to present the Indian embodied gestures and practices, values and meanings. This is to say, an effort is made to redress Indian bodies with transgressive gestures and present them as Indian, to repossess them as embodiments of a suppressed tradition and not as exotica for the tourist gaze.

As Trinh T. Min-ha states, "The West is painfully made to realize the existence of a Third World in the First World, and vice versa."[65] The Thirding as Othering. A third Space filled with the perils and possibilities that create and suck in marginalities. The third world grates against the first and bleeds. As Anzaldua writes, "before a scab forms it hemorrhages again, the lifeblood of two worlds merging to form a third country—a border culture."[66] Yet the border culture seems to be regarded as an interface of superior and inferior such that the globalizing superior tends to subject the inferior Other by lending a marginal space to it. In this sense, Indian Space, the Third space, can be judged in three ways: as subjective invention; as inadequate with respect to globalizing needs; as something to be reduced to attract gaping tourists. In all cases, the Thirding as Othering will be judged either as primitive, savage with respect to the globalizing morality, or as uncreative with respect to other phases of the global logics of subjective inventiveness. We are all the time catching up, we are the underdeveloped, poverty-ridden victims trying to be enlightened and emancipated by the Global logic. Our stuff is not good enough, the Western stuff is. . . . Thus we are asked to dress ourselves in the rhetorical garb of the globalizing West. The inadequacies of the Indian Third Space and catching up can be traced back to the time when India was colonized, especially when the space was dubbed, stereotyped as naked savage, dark and ominous, with bones in his nose and pierced earlobes, and strange figures incised into his skin.

Though the Western Space, Western artists in all fields, from painting, sculpture, music, dance, fashion, have called the Indian Space the savage primitive, but the West has learned a great deal from the so-called primitive. Today practices like henna, tattoo, scarification, barbaric clothing, practice of body arts which were deemed primitive have been transgressed into exotic, trendy, or even "cool"; they have been redressed into fashionable forms of appropriation, reinterpretation, or even misinterpretation, have gained currency and have in fact offered and inspired creative innovations. Decorating, scarification, and altering the body, traditionally was a part of every human society. "After all the body is a medium through which we most directly project ourselves in social life, our use and presentation of it say precise things about the society in which we live, the degree of our integration within that society and the controls which society exerts."[67] Body decoration serves to set people apart from one another; it was done to enhance the beauty of the body, to strengthen the healthy look. In many African and Asian societies body decoration is an integral part of the celebration of different rites of passage or a new status in life, such as birth, marriage or death. In many parts of Africa, permanent body alterations such as scarifications were often done to emphasize membership; body decoration served as a public marker of ethnicity, identity and personal allegiance to a particular group.[68]

This body art that played a crucial role in the life of Indian societies was judged primitive, immoral by the colonizers, but today with the recent shift in the art market and the new focus on exotica, and exoticism, the genre of artistic practice and scholarship has changed. In respect to the globalizing morality or with respect to other phases of the global logics of subjective inventiveness, the traditional Indian aesthetics that were regarded as primitive, savage became regarded as subjective, interest-laden expressions or social promotions of traditional Indian powerholders. This subjectivation of the Indian primitive later was drawn into the globalizing process as exotic material to be sold for a price, to be consumed as touristically exotic. In this context I portray the example of henna mania: body painting, which was called a primitive, savage act as a fashion, exotic statement today.

Henna art has been part of my growing up in the world I hail from. As an Indian, I grew up seeing intricate, elaborate designs on many women, and children around me done on festive occasions. It is an art practiced by mothers, aunts, sisters, and traditionally passed on from one generation of women to another from mother to daughter. A predominantly feminine art, done by women, especially in India, henna painting was done on the occasion which we call the "making of the bride." It is often an elaborate celebration. In fact the designs and their placements on the body distinguished the married from the unmarried. "Henna decorations worked as a social marker along with other variables as hairstyle, jewelry, costume, make-up and perfume, henna was a part of an entire aesthetic system that includes the olfactory and tactile as necessary elements."[69]

> Henna, one of the most ancient cosmetics known to human society is a paste made of dried and pulverized leaves of Lawsonia inerm, a small shrub found in Africa, Asia and Australia. Henna derives its name from Persia and has been found that ancient Egyptians used henna. Henna results in aesthetically pleasing designs ranging in color from red to dark brown or black, sometimes ointments and incense are used to create this effect. The exact shade depends on the length of time the paste is left to dry on the skin and on the extra ingredients which are added to it. Preference for henna

colors ranges from reddish brown in India and Morocco to dark brown or black in Sudan. Unlike tattooing or scarification, the process is painless and leaves no permanent trace, a major factor in its appeal to westerners. Henna is popular in India, parts of East Africa, coastal regions of Tanzania and Kenya or West African places like Senegal, Mali and Nigeria.[70]

The skin is treated like a canvas for brightly colored designs. Henna body painting is so popular in the West and has become such an exotic trend that one can walk into a retail store or a trendy body shop and buy a henna kit with step-by-step instructions and readymade designs which one traces onto the body with the henna paste. Originality and individuality are highly appreciated, although henna art is a communally oriented art form. Henna not only beautifies the skin but it also conditions the skin, it has medicinal and healing qualities. According to the mythology of ancient Hinduism, Judaism, and Islam, henna painting was done before an auspicious event mainly to protect its wearer from the evil eye as it is believed that decorating the body with henna had magical qualities to protect its wearer. In Sudan, Morocco, Pakistan, Oman, Bangladesh, and India, the tradition has been elevated to a serious art form with its own class of full-time professional artists who paint elaborate, intricate designs and they are specially hired during weddings and other auspicious occasions. Today, with henna gone global and it being an exotic trend, several artists from these countries have begun to enjoy the patronage of the rich and famous in Europe and North America.[71]

I remember the first time I encountered the craze for henna body painting, I was walking down the streets of New York City and came across a sign. I paused in front of the sign board, it read; "Look authentic, traditional, exotic get hennaed," and in small letters it also mentions "Hennaing is painless, a temporary tattoo," and "Mehndi (as we call it in India) is a timeless exotic art from the orient exotic lands of Africa and Asia." The sign board was of a body shop, where piercing and tattooing were done. Of course, I was curious to check it out and so I entered the shop; the interior of the shop I distinctly remember smelled of leather, chains, rings, hand-cuffs and in the midst was a poster authenticating the exoticism of henna painting; the poster portrayed Madonna with her hands hennaed (Fig. 2.1). Looking at this: Am I to be angry or happy that henna painting has become so hip . . . what was my feeling? I thought it is a very good marketable strategy, what a capitalist world . . . initially henna/body painting, it was a brutal savage uncivilized act. Today when a White skin appropriates it, then it becomes a fashion statement. I thought to myself, ME exotic bitch, use it, why should I be angry. The irony is, I say I am not angry, but what crossed my thoughts was where and when henna was done in India, it was always a festive event, colorful, smell of flowers and the atmosphere was of celebration but here I smelled perspiration, bikes, chains—contrasting isn't it. Henna body painting has become the latest

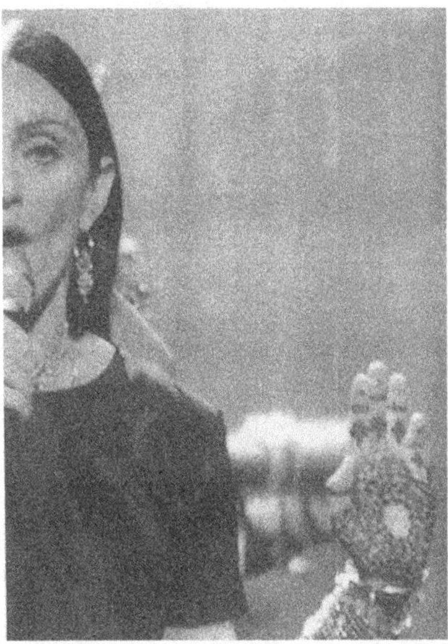

Figure 2.1. Poster (portraying Madonna with her hands hennaed). Photograph by the author of the poster from the Body Shop in New York City.

craze in the United States and the United Kingdom, especially among many icons of Western pop culture. Henna painting was often done on the hands and feet (Figs. 2.2 and 2.3), with intricate designs; now with the craze one

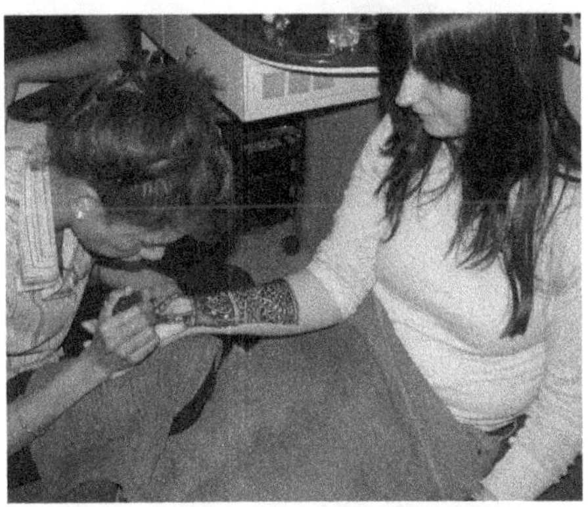

Figure 2.2. Henna painting being done by an expert henna artist. Courtesy, Ms. Perrone and the Henna Artist from the Mumbai Beauty Parlor. Photograph by the author.

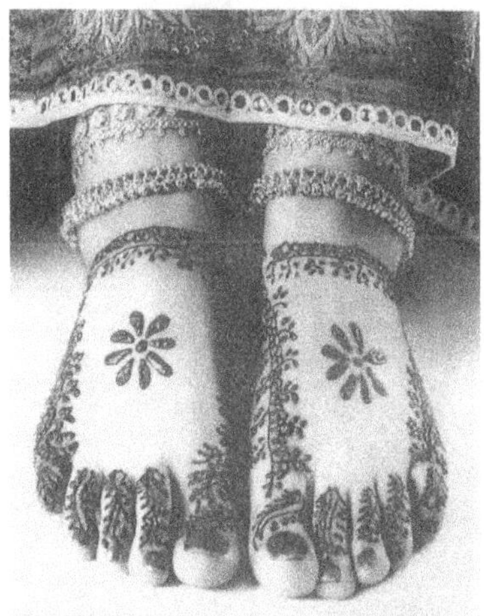

Figure 2.3. Henna painting on the feet. Photograph by the author.

notices not just hands, but backs, belly, thighs, neck and some unimaginable parts are painted with words and these are fashionable, popular as they graced the smooth, silky skin of the supermodels and Hollywood stars.

The craze of hennaing has been elevated to such a sublime dedicational level that the British singer Sting and his wife both have been known to have Zen Mehndi evenings, not to miss the Zen part of it. They hired a henna artist to decorate their guests with henna for their Zen Mehndi evenings. The Zen meditation of body painting was considered as relaxing, just imagine the heightened elevation from barbaric, savage to the spiritual. The popular icons Prince (Fig. 2.4) and Madonna have often appeared in several concerts with their hands adorned. Demi Moore, the Hollywood star, and supermodel Naomi Campbell, reported how they wore henna decorations on a regular basis. The rage is not just for supermodels and Hollywood stars, but also fashionable elite women of London and New York City who have their hands and feet and other body parts decorated with henna—of course the scenario here is not a body shop with the smell of leather and chains, but a parlor where the rich elite is catered to, with manicure and pedicure. The artists are often Sudanese and Indians. They work for an "entrepreneur, who advertises the Sudanese and Indian national origin of the artists, and by extension her closeness to the tradition of henna, coming from the ancient land and so as getting the authentic thing!"[72]

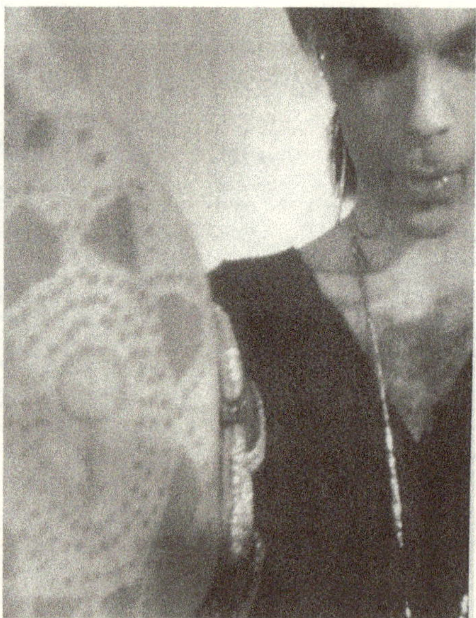

Figure 2.4. Poster (portraying Prince adorned with henna). Photograph by the author of the poster from the Body Shop in New York City.

The craze for henna has grown so much that there are television shows that demonstrate henna painting, the healthy, medicinal value of it, books are published on henna art, manuals on Do-it-Yourself, and not to mention the endless exoticism of it even in the virtual space. Today cyberspace lists the specialized features of henna painting and also there are Web sites dedicated to the art of henna. One wonders why the craze for a local tradition of India and Africa? Once considered primitive, savage, it now produces the exotic fascination—which contrasts sharply with the West's traditional contempt for non-Western people, and the mixture of desire and fear towards them. The primitive is now a current fad, an exotica. In fact, henna artists market themselves as wedding consultants or as consultants for different ceremonies; they are known for their expertise in traditional body care, like vapor bath and the burning of incense to perfume the body and many other rituals of body care. For example Setona, an international henna artist, who has become so successful, portrays the henna craze of the West. She markets herself as the "Black Magic Woman," the labeling playing to the West and their capitalization of the exotic, the magical and the primitive.[73] The mania is popular in the West as solace for their looming sense of something missing from their worldly oriented and materialistic life, "hence the appropriation of spiritual items from remote and unfamiliar places evokes a longing at the same time that it provides a justification for multiculturalism."[74] Is it justification or validation of non-Western cultural products or a demand of exoticism or is it a White man's guilt?

Cultural appropriation, misappropriation, interpretation, misinterpretation speaks and echoes the power of the dominant West, their control of media, education, and norms of acceptability and portrays their prime right to legitimize, authenticate. It is true as Sherry Chopra,[75] an Indian writer based in Canada, notes in the Ottawa Citizen editorial: "the fact that aspects of a minority culture must be first legitimized by a white person to be accepted is an example of racism. The bindhi, which for years has been ridiculed as a paki dot is now at the height of fashion, and worn by white girls and women. It is acceptable because it has been made to by white celebrities."[76] As bell hooks criticizes in her essay entitled 'Madonna, Plantation Mistress, or Soul Sister,' she characterizes stars like Madonna, the White woman, who show their interest in appropriating Black culture as "another sign of their radical chic." I agree, as hooks notes Madonna and her like speak of their envy, desire, and fascination with Blackness because the good White girls should stay away from such barbaric appropriations. This is where I have mixed feelings of henna painting or any other form of appropriation being made popular because, ideally, the concept is still uncivilized, primitive, and only because of its initial marking it is being exoticized today where the "proper" White girls stay away from. Thus this kind of "intimacy with nasty Blackness,"[77] the White fascination that they flaunt in turn destroys, redresses, consumes, commodifies, disrupts the traditional Other, disrobing the Black culture.

Disruption of Traditional Other

Traditions carry habitually established aesthetic styles, deemed to be appealing and beautiful, of high permanent value. They present stability and are recognized by scholars, critics, and members of the public by their permanent features. In many cases they acquire the reverent designation "classical." Arts that are accepted as Western classical styles in painting, music, dance show specific features that appear to be invariant, such as containment in a "frame." In addition, such styles are deemed to be creations of the geniuses of a "race," for example, European. Such classical styles are also posited as true standards of artistic creations. These standards are/were used to judge the Other in order to point out its inferiority, its being less than, and perhaps not even art.

Given a civilization that maintains its own artistic stability, the appearance of an alien style is judged in many negative ways: demonized, denigrated, assaulted, and touristically exoticized, even classicized (belonging to "lowest classes"). This is obvious from the judgments visited on henna painting, body art, scarification, tattooing and even the appearance of jazz, which was regarded as demonic, a total destruction of civilization, frameless, an intrusion from the dark and chaotic recesses of the Black soul. I call this intersection by the art of the racial other as permanence disruption. This is to say, the Indian and African arts do not follow "proper structural frames," stylistic stabilities and parameters, and hence are a threat to "real classical" art. The music has no central key, the dances are wild, the masks are distortions of "true" human form. Indeed, the arts of the "Other race" and the race itself, are regarded as parts of the natural landscape, whereas "we" are the humans who create something above nature. I show that this denigration of the "Other race" is an effort to maintain the permanence of one's own invented superior position. But to maintain this position, one engages in hermeneutics of suppression. The latter does not claim to exclude the arts of the Other, but by usurping the privilege of aesthetic criticism recontextualizes, renames, repositions, and finally, abolishes the sense of art of a given tradition. This is to say, in most cases the art works are not subjected to physical destruction; they are rearticulated in ways that make them into monsters, demonic images, expressions of immoral and indeed lesser beings. I would even state that this fate might be worse than that of complete destruction, because in the latter there are no images to show, but in the hermeneutics of suppression, the images, stories, texts, and dances are paraded in their reinterpreted fashion and thus located as the arts of the Other that have only negative designation: They are to be paraded in this reinterpreted manner as disruptions of "permanent human values," creative geniuses, and high aesthetic standards. These very arts which were disrupted as inferior Other today are of course a fad, an exotica, still an art of the Other. Not an inferior, savage Other but an Exotic Other as noted in terms of the henna body art.

This aspect of difference is not only in Black faith or Black culture, contemporary Black art or omnipotently present during British rule in India, but still present in subtle variations in the contemporary India/neocolonial India/postcolonial or for that matter everywhere the Other is the race apart from the Eurocentric "I." Even the colonized have incorporated the judgments of the colonizer concerning their own traditional arts. The colonized, in short, see with the borrowed gaze of the colonizer and, hence, pass judgments on the inadequacies of their own aesthetic traditions, on the inappropriateness of the subject matter and the use of sayings and images. For instance, whenever I visited my aunt, she would ask me if I had scrubbed myself really well so that the brown dirt (the darkness of my skin) would wash away, as I am not the fairest of all. The concept being fair, White is more beautiful, a superior race just as the British thought has rubbed on to my aunt, even though the majority of Indians are dark-skinned.

With reference to Indian sculpture, the figure of goddess Kali (Fig. 2.5) was first viewed by the British travelers as diabolic, monstrous, demonic, for she is so colossal, so huge and terrible, that there is no beauty in her size and numerous arms. The Brits said Indians don't have a clue about anatomy, they don't know how to draw and render in art the real shape of things. The British never bothered to learn; the Indian aesthetics is replete with symbolism of cosmic conceptions and not of representations of "proper" bodies. Kali was one form of *shakti*, power, force, symbolism and is encompassed within the Hindu

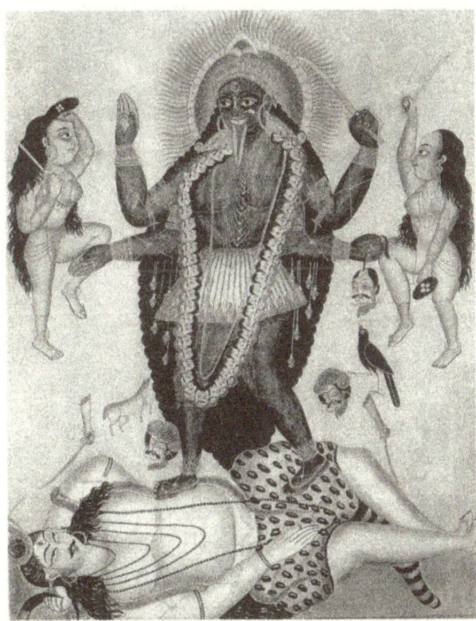

Figure 2.5. Goddess Kali. Photograph by the author.

mythology and aesthetics as the all powerful *saguna Brahman* form. She is an image of matriarchal, maternal power, force, originator, *adya shakti*, the primal energy, cosmic energy world mother. Cosmic energy in its dynamic form is symbolized in the form of *shakti*, the world mother, who is power and energy by which the creation, preservation and destruction of the world, universe is portrayed in this all encompassing form.

Stereotyped notions of the goddess Kali haunt the European mind, as can be seen in the observations by Geoffery Moorehouse in his book *Calcutta*: "The very name of Calcutta is derived from the symbol of fear and evil." He writes, "all representations of Kali are designed to frighten an illiterate and superstitious mind. . . . She appears with devilish eyes, or with tongue dripping blood, with snakes entwined round her neck or with a garland of skulls."[78] The form, image is completely misinterpreted not only by the British at that time, but also today in different tones of transgressions. For example, the portrayal of Kali in the 1984 Hollywood movie *Indiana Jones and the Temple of Doom*, is as a demoness, grotesque, macabre, wherein to appease her the so-called Indian priests tear out hearts of innocent children to offer to the goddess, who is depicted as a blood-sucking, terrible idol. Imagine such distorted depictions, what cross-cultural understanding would the Westerners face. Another example I recall is a poster (Fig. 2.6) that I saw in Athens, Ohio, in a bar; it was a poster for a rock concert depicting a ferocious, terrible Kali as the symbol for their band. I was amused and amazed, I thought Kali has become

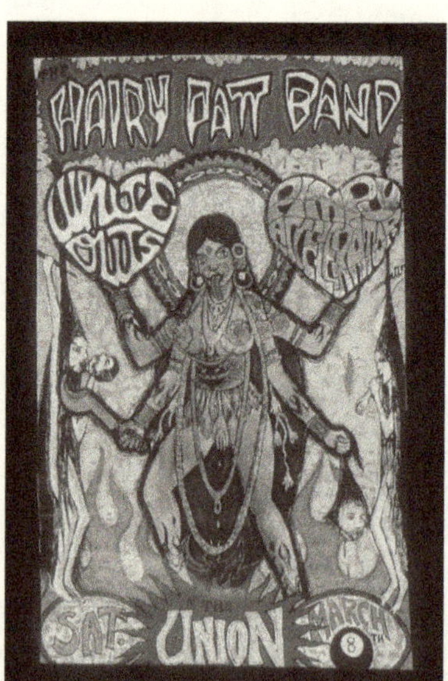

Figure 2.6. Poster for a rock concert. Photograph by the author.

exotic and chic. How can one miss, the *Sex Goddess*, Annie Sprinkle (the postporn modern artist), Tantric inspired cosmic Kali (Fig. 2.7), Sprinkle as the Neo Sacred Prostitute/Goddess. She is known as the prostitute and porn star turned sex educator and artist. Sprinkle's work has always been about sexuality, with a political, spiritual, and artistic bent. Goddess Kali, the all-powerful omnipotent maternal being, has become so popular, exotic, that she has also been adorned by the porn star—what more inspiration of Indianness can one ask for. Should I praise her for her ingenuity of adorning herself as Kali with the multiple arms? Instead of the goddess holding icons/weapons in her hand, she holds the sex toys. Sprinkle says, "Sex is a path to enlightenment. . . ." She celebrates sex as a nourishing, life-giving force, she describes her work as an inspiration from Eastern philosophy, yoga, meditative breathing, spirituality and healing. Ironic isn't it; Kali who was diabolic, monstrous during colonial times is now a seductress oozing with exotic sexuality paraded in the world of porn as a neosacred prostitute; either way one can note whether it is by Sprinkle's work, or the colonial/postcolonial interpretation, the goddess Kali is transgressed/disrobed of her sacred cosmic maternal essence.

This same colonizing and self-colonizing appears in the manner in which the Indian sculptures at Khajuraho (discussed in the previous chapter) (Fig. 2.8)

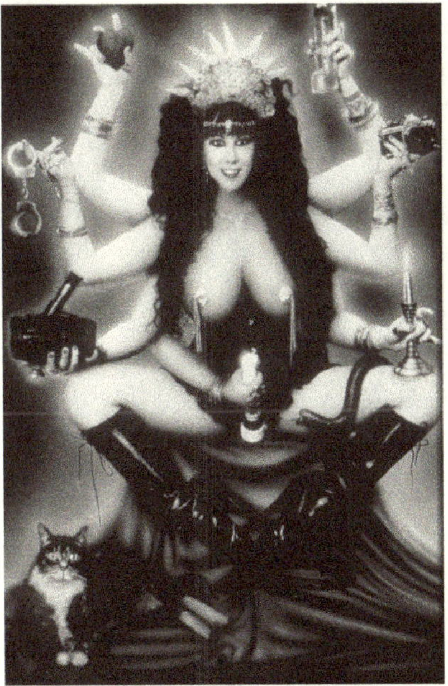

Figure 2.7. Annie Sprinkle as the neo sacred prostitute/goddess. Photo Credit, Amy Audrey. Courtesy Annie Sprinkle.

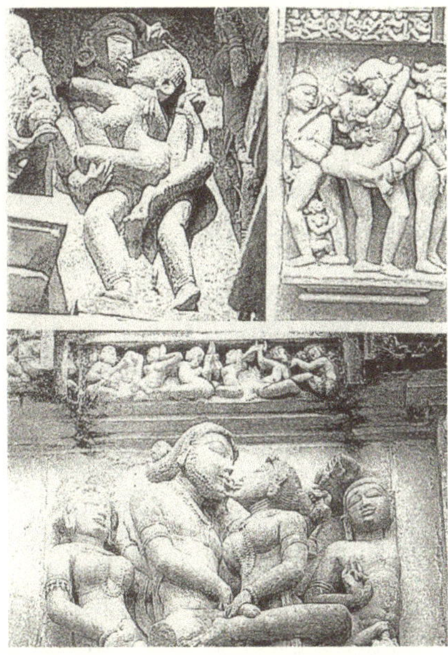

Figure 2.8. *Mithuna* sculptures. Khajuraho. Photograph by the author.

were and are viewed. These beautiful, immense sculptures, which portrayed the cosmic-*kamic*, love, union, were thoroughly misinterpreted and taken out of Hindu context by being called pornographic. The carved imagery is designed to articulate the *kamic*, erotic connection of all events, things, mythical figures without social gradations. They form, so to speak, an entire universe connected by erotic attraction. Yet, this blissful cosmic nexus is denigrated as the art of the inferior Other and, hence, located in the unspeakable and uncivilized region of immorality, sexual promiscuity, bestiality, and hence, is deemed not deserving the title of art. The colonial period, indeed, brought the question of morals, moralizing, gender, and genderising issues into art:

> The British even said the sculptures at Khajuraho were extremely indecent, obscene and offensive specially to find them in the temples that professed to be erected for good purposes on account of religion; everywhere there are a number of female figures who are represented dropping their clothes and thus purposely exposing their persons.[79]

The British regarded these aesthetic images as indecent and obscene, and thus to be judged morally and not aesthetically. Once again, the significant aspect of this art, its cosmic nexus, the cosmic union, the cosmic aesthetics is excluded and thus inserted into an entirely different context. The way of looking at sexuality is perceived as something different, excessive, Other. These images are aestheticized "thinghood," and the body is projected as nexus of exotic sexual fantasies about the Indian body. Approached as a textual system, the bodies point to an erotic, hypersexual aesthetic objectification of bodies as an idealized form of homogeneous type, thoroughly saturated with a totality of sexual predicates. The cosmic energies that symbolize both creative and destructive forces impinged on British imagination the wildest proclivities of India and the Indians.

For the British, the Indians evidenced depravity and intimacy, the forces of darkness. Such imaginings of the cosmic energies were viewed by the British as ritualized sexuality, suggesting that Indians should be feared as subjects who had the dark forces playing as perverts, threatening to invade and seduce, rape the White world. A visitor to India during the 1930s was warned by a seasoned British woman: 'You'll never understand the dark and tortuous minds of the natives . . . and if you do I shan't like you—you won't be healthy.'[80] The British women found their safest course was to barricade themselves within their own community, to shield their consciousness against India's immoral encroachment: "Hold ye the Faith—the Faith our Fathers sealed us; / Whoring not with visions—oversize and overstale" (Kipling, "A Song of the English").[81] The view I would say has not changed today only the tone; instead of "dark forces as perverts" now they are "dark forces as exotica," and they still desire and are threatened by the dark exotica. The desire is often portrayed as the radical chic appropriated by popular icon images from Hollywood or by supermodels and is sold as the exotic capitalizing and disrupting the traditional Other (as discussed before).

The art of the Other, just as the difference of the Other, is held to belong to the natural landscape, but not to be art. The images, just as the native naked bodies, are judged on the grounds of morality, that is, lack of cultural elevation, and hence as belonging to mere nature. After all, the very term *native* suggests that those so designated live merely naturally. Thus, in the hermeneutics of the Other's art and the Other, objectified as inferior, supremacy and power are given, in turn, to the phallocentric White man whose flesh becomes burdened with the task of symbolizing the transgressive fantasies and desires of the White Western male subject. Thus, he must float the Western logic as the superior image, even for the neocolonials. As Homi Bhabha has suggested, "an important feature of colonial discourse is its dependence on the concept of fixity in the ideological constructions of otherness."[82] Looking at these examples and broadening this theme, one can see that representations of the hermenuetics of the Other in Western culture entail different degrees of Othering or, as it were, different practices of representations of the Othering, that is, different positions of identification on the part of the White subject.

Appropriation, redressing can work, in another manner, to reemphasize, subvert or portray ironic self-referentiality, for example alluding to henna painting (Fig. 2.9), Shirin Neshat, an Iranian-born New York-based artist explores in her work "Guardians of Revolution" (Women of Allah Series), "Birth Mark,"

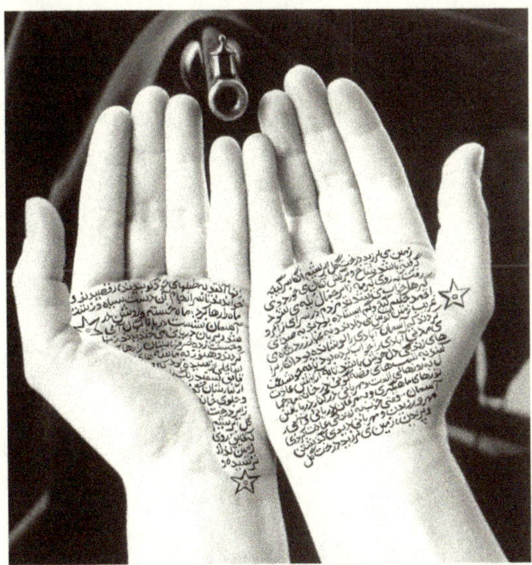

Figure 2.9. Shirin Neshat. *Guardians of Revolution (Women of Allah series)*, 1994. B&W RC print & ink. © Shirin Neshat. Courtesy Gladstone Gallery.

"Identified" and "Stories of Martyrdom," the poetry drawn through textual calligraphy inscribed on their faces, hands, and feet in a manner reminiscent of henna decorations. She critically portrays how a "woman's body has been a type of battleground for various kinds of rhetoric and political ideology." "The renewed interest in henna body art in the West offers an unique opportunity to reflect on artistic practices in this age of massive mobility, dislocation and globality. It causes one to rethink traditional conceptions of art and aesthetics, perceptions of the body, the culture of sex and desire and above all fashion as a statement and public display of the self."[83]

The interest is not just in henna body art, but also in the primitive, savage designs, patterns, textiles, spicy hot cuisine, curries, the Indian music, rhythm, as it is called the Indian *taal*, beat. The *bhangra, Punjabi*, music that has a fast beat is used in the gym by the aerobic instructor, Sarina Jain (discussed in the previous chapter). The leading fashion designers present collections that are called the Indian-inspired clothing designs and accessories in which beads and leather are combined and embellished with crystals and glitter. Should one say tradition versus modernity or exoticism? For example, in the United Kingdom, specifically in London and Leeds, I saw a boutique that had an entire collection of Indian clothes and accessories called the *Exotic Monsoon Wedding Collection* inspired after the Hindi movie, *Monsoon Wedding* (Fig. 2.10). Fashion designers emphasize traditional patterns taken from—or as they call it—borrowed from Mumbai, creating beaded, sequined patterns as fashion statements (Fig. 2.11), where they feel they are imparting and reflecting, redressing the Indian tradition and sensibilities.

With reference to the different artists' work, Indian space, one can note that, in principle, or eidetically speaking, the world of aesthetics, especially

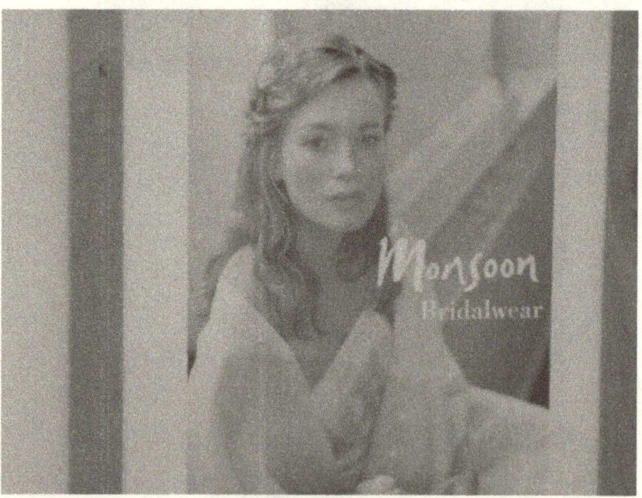

Figure 2.10. *Exotic Monsoon Wedding Collection.* Photograph by the author.

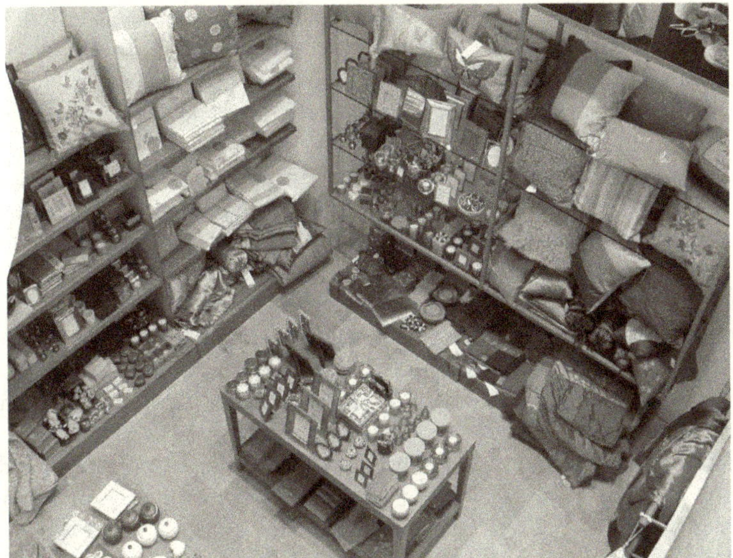

Figure 2.11. Beaded, sequined patterns. Photograph by the author.

the aesthetics of contemporary Indian art, the Indian space, art of the immigrant artists, encompasses ambivalent expressivities. The colonially modified ways, the traditional dressing, are the irrepressible forces which pervade contemporary India, neocolonial Indians and Indians in western Cities. One can note nevertheless the appropriation and redressing that was constituted. The question is can a tradition be reclaimed? There is a search within, but the search gets trapped by the questions of tradition/modernity, local/global, identity/exotica. Internationally, Indian contemporary art is gaining in recognition, but the question is, what kind of Indian art? Just as the growing popularity centered on Gandhi, *gurus*, yoga, sati, dowry, curries, *mehndi*, henna, *chai*, tea, primitive, savage, the art, which is catered to, is the exotica, the exoticism of India. Such is the trap, the exotica of the Indian Space. Traversing through tradition, modernity, coming to the present contemporaneity, we ask: Where are we today? Do we know?

As Fred Pfeil notes:

For who among us, after all—white or nonwhite, western or not—is not always caught precisely in the space between 'inherited traditions' and 'modernizations projects'? And where else, how else, do 'cultural interpretations' come from—'theirs' or 'ours,' local or global, resistant or complicit, as the case may be—other than from the spaces between the two, and with the ensemble of materials they provide, or forced to provide and thus open a space that is negative.[84]

I reflected on this quote and thought about myself, an Asian, Indian, my work, my education, and even my creative process where the loss of cultural innocence is deemed unavoidable. I cannot but assume this inescapable context that colonialism has introduced, forming the Other and therefore the Indian, and with it the Indian Third Space, leaving no choice but to remain in this Space, always striving to catch up. In turn, the colonialist, and myself as a postcolonial artist and scholar, and at present residing in the States equally, have no choice but to take the other into account: we have an interpretive context that the two belong to each other. Although this context exists even for me, me being a colonial body, I have acquired an awareness of the subjugating force of my own postcolonial being and, therefore, I am in a position to open up the difference between my tradition and the colonial presence that allows me to rearticulate both. Although I cannot choose not to choose, because I now face the options and attempt to make sense of it all, I find myself constantly facing the questions, Who am I? What am I to create in order to note the difference, and the mutual otherness, between my tradition, and my postcolonial self? Can I recloth the texture of my skin, or shall I wear it with the marks inscribed by the Other?

The Scars of the Past

Inscription in the Dwelling of my Skin
The bitter cry
The desire for an 'I'
Bad faith still lurks
It is always the question????
Can I choose not to choose as I face the options . . .
The fallacy exists, exists even for me
The veil is thin between **Black, Brown and White**
The colors do they matter
Sure they are unveiled in public
Can we see Beyond
Black/Brown is Beautiful, Exotic
Is the slogan Today
It's on everyone's Lips
The feline, raw savage Beauty
Enjoy it, parade it
Redress, Recloth . . .
Let the White Desire more **Blackness**

—*Rekha Menon*

Vacillating Morality

POPULAR LIBRARY

SHE WAS SEDUCTIVE AND DANGEROUS

TALES OF

Indian Exotic Bitch

Menon Rekha

Ten stories of macabre
mystery by the creator of
the famous Dr. Fu Manchu

3

Desirous Seduction

The Irony of Desirous Seduction in Bollywood Films

Setting the scene:
Unveiling
   Unmasking
      Disrobing
         Imprisoned
               Its me
                  a woman
                        do I know, should I know, can I know
When lives are pitched to the buying and selling of desire
     Insatiable desire
        The irony
I unveiled you
   Unmasked you
      Your desire
         Or my desire
Where am I, do I know
They can smell my blood
Its too late
Calling out my name
I am the black sheep
Crawling up my spine
I see your eyes
Could have I stopped them
From holding me down
It is too oo late now
They unveiled me
   Unmasked me
Veiling me again

Unfolding
Pulling back velvet curtains
Exposing a stage
Reveal llll peeling back layers
That surround the body iesss
The irony of desirous seduction
The visceral tactile body
The literal stage
Who am I, do I know
Lights on . . . lights on . . . black out

The discourses that are seen to pervade Bollywood films: nationalism, terror-ism, patriotism, the abuse of wealth or its legitimate pursuit, the fulfillment of personal desire, filial duties. "These discourses have frequently invoked a dichotomy between so-called tradition and supposed modernity only to subsume the latter within the former,"[85] or in an ironic fashion, it is always the women who tend to be designated as the culture-bearers and given the burdensome responsibility of preserving traditional values and aesthetics. A great salable advertisement in this context (mentioned in the previous chapter) in India is a matrimonial column where ads for brides read: "High caste, Gujarati Hindu handsome boy, English-speaking, green card, well settled in United States, with Western values invites matrimonial proposals from slim, fair, traditional Indian Hindu Brahmin girls, who adhere to traditional Indian values and customs." So it is not just in Bollywood films, in fact the films play a crucial role in ideological image building.

They work by depicting for instance heroes who are western educated going back to India to seek a traditional, docile Indian bride or portraying heroines whose lifestyles are from rich, Westernized, consumerist, urban society but whose hearts are rooted in traditional, meaning Indian values. The vir-gin heroines often are shown to push themselves to sacrifice their individual desires for the sake of their families. This epitome is emphatically played out, expressed in hyped fashion through emotional concerns, anxieties concerning family values, pure Indian values, public morality, duties, intermingling even caste, religion, and also an exploration of national identity and ideology. The myth that India remains the space for wholesome purity and it is the duty of the female to maintain and guard the so-called Indian purity. This is the irony of desirous nostalgic seduction portrayed in Bollywood films.

For example, in Subhash Ghai's *Taal*, which was so popular in the United States and in India, the film projected a sense of the so-called Indianness to the diaspora. The film presented its heroine with Indian traditional roots, but she also discovers modern realities—advertently portraying the effect of West-ern civilization on Indian culture and how the purity is being tainted with modernity;[86] the irony of course is, it is the Indian woman who is tainted if she is Westernized/modernized. Another film of Subash Ghai, *Pardes*, which was marketed with the slogan "American dream, Indian soul," consoled so many Indians who have never crossed the seven seas, reassuring them for having been a prudent Indian, nationalist who has never left home.[87] Even in this movie the heroine epitomizes the Indianness, Indian purity, values, she is even named as *Ganga* meaning metaphorically like the pure eternal river. The film stresses what the father-in-law states *"aaj ganga jaisi hee betiyan hamari ek matr ummeed hain"*—today it is daughters like Ganga who are the only hope. So the women end up carrying the burden of national tradition, duties not just in the films but also often in real life—remember the matrimonial advertisement—wanted: fair traditional Hindu bride.

This dichotomy exits not only today but even when the British ruled India, the patriarchy was not even questioned. The maternal force, the *adya shakti*, primal energy, was replaced by the so-called objectivist reading of history of an omnipotent patriarchy. Despite the *Shaktic* texts, the glorification of the maternal the goddess, the primal feminine energy, the *matram*, the measure, the *matrika*, mother, the power, the originator was ignored, gradually losing any vitality it once had, first becoming invisible and then finally lost to a construction of paradigms created by a male-dominated, patriarchal caste. The heteropatriarchal order, or the ideological construction of overpowering patriarchy, was not even questioned. It became the universalized truth. Even discourses postulating clear rules on how stories ought to be written and interpreted, as well as the selectivity of myths, the mode of narration and fixing of word meanings, allowed the heteropatriarchal ideology to be elaborated through various textual and mythical traditions.[88] The 19th-century nationalist and colonialist discourses both provide, "for a construction of Hindu identity on the basis of a glorious *Aryan* heritage, which privileged the *Vedic*, *brahamanic* and *kshatriya* traditions, where women were made into true Hindu women, who was either a wife or a mother, faithful to her men and nation, and the masculine identity of the Hindu man was the superior heroic warrior, true manhood, *virya*."[89] *Shaktic* traditions were ignored, even if they were practiced, and when women were allowed to move out of their domesticity, they still remained under the male tutelage.[90]

The Hindu woman was the epitome of Hindu spirituality, in contrast to western materialism; in the words of Vivekananda, ". . . a well educated girl in shameless freedom . . . has arousing desires . . . and the scene changes and there appears in place stern presence Sita, Savitri . . .":[91]

The West is constructed through images of the educated, shameless girl, prey to arousing desires and is juxtaposed to the image of the spiritual East through the vanquishing of desire. Both poles are constructed on the woman's body and her desires. Freedom, education, giving in to desires become conflated with western materialism whereas self sacrifice and chastity become associated with eastern spirituality. Within this discourse the superiority of the eastern morality is demonstrated by the responsibility of the Indian woman as the eternal sacrificer, the victim who willingly chooses to sacrifice herself.[92]

Nationalism was never ungendered, so also today India is not ungendered. "the boundaries of a nation are drawn on the bodies of women," just as for Gandhi motherhood was the ultimate form of womanhood.[93] For Viveknanda, "chaste motherhood represented the secret of the race. . . . In India the mother was center of the family, she the mother of the universe, is the representative of God, . . . Our god is personal and absolute . . . the absolute is the male and the personal the female. . . ."[94]

Thus, one sees the changes occurring from maternal force to motherhood, woman as the chaste mother . . . that is how it is even today in contemporary India. The male is the overpowering patriarchal heterosexual power, the vital, and the woman is the sexual innocent. The male is the phallus incarnate with distinct elements of the flasher who needs constant reassurance by the woman of his power, intactness, a woman who melts into submission and longing. Sitas's legend—Sita the heroine of the epic Ramayana, is being interpreted keeping in mind the Hindu imagery of manliness—is often emphasized as the promotion of an ideal of womanhood, one of chastity, purity, gentle tenderness, and singular faithfulness, the quintessence of wifely devotion. Another masculinist definition of ideals and images of women is emphasized; it is taken from the *Laws of Manu*, which stress the need to control women because of the evils of the female character. Here are a few excerpts from the duties of women: A young girl, woman, or aged one, must not do anything independently. In childhood she must be subject to her father, in youth to her husband, and when her Lord is dead to her sons. Though destitute of virtue or devoid of good qualities, seeking pleasure elsewhere, yet a husband must be constantly worshipped as Lord. She should control her thoughts and never violate her husband, only then will she be a virtuous wife.[95] These are the versions which are remembered and exercised. The *Shaktic* texts are conveniently forgotten in the patriarchal society.

Thus, the constructs of femininity and motherhood were reflected on and exercised to suit both the patriarchy and the nationalist movement. Just as the British rule and the Western values were allocated to the material domain, the latter was contrasted to the spiritual traditional domain, which was seen as the representative of the true identity of the Indian people, and the woman was supposed to be the guardian of this spiritual domain. As for the nationalists, this domain represented the culture and Indianness of the people and marked the superiority of Hindu as compared to the alien culture. This also projected and facilitated the Indian man's efforts to prove his masculinity in the external domain and maintained traditional patriarchal relations within the family by offering no threat to the dominance of male attitudes.[96] The lack of masculinity was a pertinent issue around which India's unfitness for self-rule and the need for the British rule were justified by colonial officials.[97] In this context it was essential for nationalist leaders to project femininity in ways which would enhance the masculine or worldly virtues of Indian men. Motherhood was also considered by nationalist leaders as an important vehicle to convey the idea of a strong civilization to the British. The idea of motherhood was identified with motherland or *Bharat mata* and as Mother India it was projected as ultimate mother.

Our great nationalist leader Gandhi, for example, encouraged women's political participation, yet he was careful that their activities did not threaten men's masculinity in any way. He excluded woman from the first salt *satyagraha* on April 6, 1930. He said that, "just as Hindus do not harm a cow, and it would be cowardice to take a cow to the battlefield, in the same way it would be cowardice for us to have woman accompany us."[98] Many nationalist woman, as well as men, subscribed to a posited dichotomy between the material West and the spiritual East, such that nationalist women often embraced their roles as repositories of a national spiritual essence who must remain untainted by Westernization and its implied pollution.[99] The home was the principal site for expressing the spiritual quality of the national culture, "and woman must take the main responsibility of protecting and nurturing this quality." No matter what the changes in the external condition of life for women, "they must not lose their essential spiritual, i.e., feminine virtues, they must not, in other words, become essentially westernized."[100] Thus the mythical figures of Sita and Savitri were considered the epitome of ideal Indian womanhood and Kali was the bad, terrible mother

A classic example of this is Sudhir Kakar's work on Indian sexuality: "he sees the main psycho-sexual problem in male children as the work of the 'bad mother' or the sexually devouring phallic woman."[101] The Kali spectrum of goddesses, the *apsaras*, embody this aspect of the overwhelming sexual mother. For Khakar, the male child feels castrated by his mother like the *Apsara*, the female vampire, who sucks the blood and lures men from their spiritual life substance.[102] Another aspect as mentioned before would be the example of tradition, where significantly, it is the women who tend to be designated as the culture-bearers and given the burdensome responsibility of preserving traditional values and aesthetics. And to remind you again, this is obvious in India in matrimonial columns where the ads for brides read, "Wanted a traditional, very fair slim woman who has traditional Indian values, customs, coming from a reputed Hindu family, for a green card Indian fair handsome boy, 26/180/65 M.Tech Software Engr. *Vaisnava, Madhesiya* community residing in United States, well settled in United States and adapted to Western lifestyle of living and Western social values." Here one can see the patriarchal power: The male can accommodate to the West but the female should continue to be subjected to the position allotted to her by her "traditional" role and maintain the spiritual, that is, feminine virtues; they must not, in other words, become essentially Westernized.

Other examples show equally the subordination of genderized woman: the dowry deaths, where the woman is abused, even burned. She exists merely as an economic asset, for she brings the dowry and is a vessel for procreation. At the least she is either a servant or, at best, one who relieves the mother-in-law of her most strenuous physical tasks. Weddings are like cattle shows where bridegrooms are bought, and on marriage, if female fetuses are suspected, they are aborted. The woman is viewed by the Indian men as a feminine principle who should be docile, innocent, domesticated, the ideal; if she is the opposite, a strong personality, then she is viewed as treacherous, lustful, and rampant with insatiable contaminating sexuality. As Kakar pointed out, she is the presence of the "bad mother," the Kali that looms in front of male children. Is it, then, a wonder what happened to the maternal force, the *Shakti*, the primal energy, the *adya shakti*, the maternal power, the all powerful *Shakti*?

This is the ideological construct which is often portrayed in the Bollywood films even today. For example, in footage from the movie *Kha Na Pyar Hai* directed by Rakesh Roshan—one can see the scene where the heroine is surveyed as an object of desire, which is offered to us even as close-ups of parts of her face as well as the heroes face as he surveys her. She, the heroine is portrayed in Western/modernized clothing but when the hero notes and mentions that simplicity, meaning Indianness read as traditional dressing is what represents as beautiful, then one notes in the very next scene the heroine dressed in traditional Indian clothing. Here, one can note how wearing traditional clothing is remarked and sold as the proper Indian womans' attire. This nevertheless portrays the desirous as the very efforts at destruction of the *adya shakti*; the feminine is also portrayed as the signification of power. No matter what the patriarchy did, it could not suppress the *shaktic* power; her excess over all limitations always appears. The more that patriarchy is against the *Shakti* power, the more the power of the maternal is reappearing. One does not get rid of the other; and the conqueror only places the defeated into a lower, darker, threatening, demonic, terrifying region. The forms of the other are caricatured, made grotesque and always located in the nether regions, but still they haunt the purported "higher" civilization. Not only haunt, but at times reassert their presence.

For example, in the movie *Satta*, the dichotomy played out is one of the dominant representations which celebrate the dynamism, reclaiming empowerment and self-definition of the maternal in woman's image, which is portrayed with a selfish interest of the father-in-law/patriarchy in order not to loose the constituency seat. He asks her to take his son's seat/place, for his son is not allowed to contest elections because of his murder trial and the uproar of being caught for rape. The woman is shown as powerful and she, the heroine, takes over, dominates towards the end of the movie although earlier on she is shown as an impure woman scorned for not being docile by the same person, father-in-law. *Satta* plays out the moral ambiguities of contemporary India. The neocolonialist concept of morality vacillates colored by the Victorian moral codes.

Another movie, *Mr. And Mrs. Iyer*, directed by Aparna Sen portrays the communal tension in present day India. In this movie one can note how one is bound by customs—the so-called customs or as the neocolonial would say the so-called Hindu tradition. Hinduism, not being a religion, is, in fact, part of the Western vocabulary that the Hindu fundamentalists accept. In this sense, they are within the context of the bifurcated consciousness that is revealed in their anger and their wish. My point is that the very secular political institutions of India are subverted by Hindu traditionalists who are completely imbued with British colonial attitudes—the British prudish Victorian morality. This concept, director Deepa Mehta has beautifully captured and portrayed in the films *Fire* (discussed in the previous chapter) and *Earth*.

In the movie *Earth*, Mehta artfully relays an historical event, the partition of India in a very intimate, emotional and a feminine way. I say *feminine* because she has opened up aspects that others wouldn't like—woman's sexuality, woman's place in society or even the fear of women's power, or the maternal presence; these were wonderfully portrayed in her previous film *Fire*. Mehta composes her films in terms of elements: fire, earth, and both are maternal, one deals with feminine passion, life and the other, *Earth*, deals with the source of everything. Nationalism was never ungendered, nor was the partition, so also India today is not ungendered. One encounters in Mehta's films the boundaries of a nation that are drawn on the bodies of women. Even in *Earth*, one can note how it is the women who are violated, the kernel is destroyed and Earth being the maternal presence/the mother, who is the source of life, death and regeneration, is the one to be divided, the fragmentation takes place and patriarchy rules. Earth the maternal is the One, who contains all the cosmic forces from *Shakti*/power, energy, strength to *Kama*/love, desire *lila* and hence has no preferences for specific religion, but yet it is the earth the maternal that is partitioned in the name of religion. It is so difficult to look back and think that to begin with Hinduism was not even a religion, it was just a way of life, and how today one has completely forgotten that aspect; nobody even remembers that it is a way of life. Hinduism became a religion, through overpowering patriarchy, colonial interpretation, and the British using the religion as a tool to divide. It is also interesting to note Mehta's artistry in portraying how the societies get transformed; different people go about doing and being involved in different occupations and they still mingle and live together in innocent harmony. This innocence is disrupted, shattered by the intervention not only of the British but also the beastiality/animal instincts which sleeps dormant inside us and once the cage opens, we shower our destructive fury and destroy the peace and innocence is sacrificed.

The movie portrays the conflict between India and Pakistan that started even before India's independence. Gandhi went on a hunger strike to stop the battles between Hindus and Muslims and he did manage to stop the conflict for that period. At the time of independence, he gave in to Jhina, the leader of the Muslim party. He failed and agreed to the partition between India and Pakistan. The Earth/land was divided on the basis of India as a majority of Hindus, and Pakistan as the majority of Muslims, then one wonders wasn't Gandhi mistaken to proclaim that we are all children of the same God. Gandhi's efforts to unify under one god did not recognize the difference between "religions" hence, Muslims have a very different conception of the ultimate than Hindus. This conflict is still going on, in fact the relationship between India and Pakistan today is very tense. The intricacies of the narration, the artistry of the film notes the earth not only as the maternal, the mother, the women, as the final transgressors of *dharma*/righteousness.

In the world of film, Bollywood does capture, vacillate morality, and portray transgressions of masculinity and femininity. The emotive modalities often presenting and reinforcing the traditional role of an Indian woman, in spite of the erotic seduction—therein lies the irony of the nostalgia of the so called Indian tradition. The movies do encourage tradition as the dominant role, warn of the dangers of nonconformity, but then globalization creeps in to be sucked into the dissidence of tradition.

The Globalization of Indian Marriages

Three Minutes: The Question of Compatibility, Death of Knowing

Three Years to Three Minutes—Does One really know the Other
It took three years for One to say I don't know You, You don't fit
    into the family. . . . Marrying You is a risk, a chance. . . .
You don't know me? I am the same person, I haven't changed in
    three years,
It took you three years to say, to realize that I don't fit into the
    family. . . .
How ironic it is. . . .

But on the other hand—these days it takes 3 minutes to decide whether the person is compatible or not, 3 minutes, as they call it today in the mobile world/culture. "Speed-dating," 3 minutes to check out if the person is compatible—is this compatibility or is it death of knowing, this is the Global world, the Global Communication today, the globalization of Indian marriages—arranged marriages get a little rearranging.

The fluidity and ubiquity of information has increased with media markets, the development of information technology, the intimated link Web sites, the millions currently with Internet access and being regular Internet users. Information has sparked a revolution, transforming lives and lifestyles, has crossed national boundaries, enabled new relations, formed new cultures, and new customs incorporating traditional Asian imaginaries.[103]

> These cultures foreground the historicity of the mediascapes of the West, Asia, and the Asian diaspora. They are characterized by the ephemerality of the commodity in late modernity. And they form networks connected by the technology of a speed-space, producing mobile and transient cultures. *Time Magazine* reported in March 2001 that in the past five years the Internet had done to Asian communities what Stonewall enabled in the West over the past twenty-five years. The 1994 introduction of the Netscape browser has played an important role in the types of information constitutive of emergent identities in Asia, its diaspora, and its cyberspace. Beginning with a handful of file transfer (ftp) sites publishing bibliographic resources about Asian literature and teleports hosting local bulletin boards, the user friendly interface has transformed information from subcultural data to a presentness enabled by multimedia synergy. With it, the interactive chats, self-managing listservs, and short messaging codes have proliferated on the bandwith alongside repertories and libraries of image worlds and signs. Information, consumption had fueled information production and an increasing self-awareness, shifting subterranean bulletin board cultures and self-writing historiographies from shared interest minority groups and genealogical retrieval to a larger project of self-creatiom.[104]

This development introduces new identities, asks questions, creates, modernizes connectivity ontologically and epistemologically. Asians use new media to challenge the traditional customs so to speak by indigenizing the global and producing mobile and contingent practices of self-inscription and self-identification.[105] The mobile culture discourse transcends all borders. This globalization has highlighted the mediated process of traditional Indian marriages. New modes and grids have been created for navigation of choosing and selecting a match. There are sites like Indianmatches.com or Indianmatrimonial.com or sites that make it even more specific to a particular caste/community, like Tamilmatch.com, the browsers with different clicks drag icons to reveal the junctions and disjunctions where meanings crack, collide, and collude. In spite of the commercialization of net-order brides to bride grooms online, the media has caught on with the Asians, Indians where it has become a crucial site for constituting new relationships, marriages, identities, and communities. These links and sites foreground intricate interactions of local and global emphasizing the local appropriation of Indian indigenous tradition of a globally mobile technology and discourse.

The availability of the Internet has changed the concept of matrimony and even the process leading to matrimony. This new media, the mobility emphasizes the local cultural traditions and reconstitutes what counts as tradition. For example, the arranged marriages get a little rearranged, new rules are formulated for old practices. The newspaper matrimonial advertisements are shifted to a virtual space and have a faster pace. The Web sites have taken over the duty of the marriage brokers. Though of course unlike the marriage brokers who do the matchmaking, here more often it is the individual, the personal self who looks at the profile that is posted at these match.com sites and checks for the compatibility. This trend, there is definitely a freedom, flexibility for the individual to match one's desire and taste. The downside of it is that the identity and who one is truly can be camouflaged.

The newspaper matrimonial advertisements often portray an example of tradition, where significantly, as discussed before, it is the women who tend to be designated as the culture bearers. These newspaper ads now have shifted to a virtual space where more often the individual or the parents post the profile. The ads (Figs. 3.1, 3.2, and 3.3) have a similar tone, only a little more elaborate with asides featured in the profile as different interests, hobbies, and so on, and of course the faster pace and the variety of choices to thread along. In the virtual space matrimonial ads, the women definitely have more freedom; they can have a choice to push the boundaries of tradition, reshape them and still remain anonymous until one is sure of the catch.

There are young, hip, South Asians who float between two cultures carefully selecting from the West to modernize the East. These young Indians push the cultural boundaries created by their parents and grandparents one step further; they are reshaping the tradition of arranged marriages. Before the mobile culture, couples were introduced by relatives and friends. Today, the boom of Web sites, chat rooms, personal ads, South Asian speed dating (especially in the United States, Britain and Canada) have caught on and the relatives are nudged out. Hindus one night, Muslims the next, men and women meet for three minutes at the bars or restaurants before moving on to the next potential mate.

Arranged marriages are still the norm; parents have become more liberal and open in their concept of marriage and courtship especially within the tight-knit communities in Britain and the United States. The nature of the

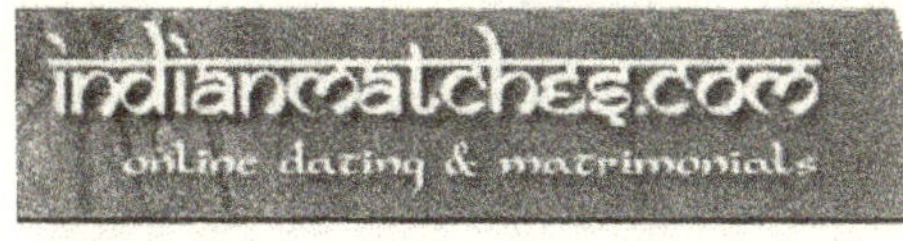

Search
· Simple Search
· Advanced Search
· Keyword Search
· Handle Search
· Profile ID Search
· Men w/ photos
· Women w/ photos
· Featured Profiles
· Who's Online
· Contact List

Quick Links
· Register
· My Home
· Search
· My Profile
· Support

Punjabi Software professional settled in Dallas

Last Activity: Within 3 months

>> Profile details   >> Send a contact message to me now
>> Desired Match   >> Introduce yourself to me
                            >> Bookmark my profile
                            >> Add my profile to your contact list

Gender:	Male
Age:	30
Relationship:	Unspecified
Height & Weight:	5 '7, 150lbs
Body Type:	Athletic
Location:	United States / Dallas, Texas
Birth Country:	India
Will Travel:	Within Any Distance
Religion:	Hindu, Somewhat religious
Cultural Values:	East & West Mix
Star Sign:	Libra
Caste/Subcaste:	Brahmin, Punjabi
Skin Tone:	Fair
Languages:	Hindi, Punjabi
Occupation:	Computers
Education:	Masters
Income:	50-100K (US)
Diet:	Non-Vegetarian
Drinker:	Drink occasionally
Smoker:	Dont Smoke
Citizenship:	Indian / H1B
Living Status:	Live Alone
Marital Status:	Never Married
Has Children:	0
Wants Children:	Yes
Health:	Healthy and fit.
Hobbies:	Music, travelling, sports

Email Profile

email this profile to a relative
or friend now!

< Enter Email >

press <enter> to send

contact now (?)

contact later (?)

Profile Details

I am 30,Punjabi Brahmin , working in Dallas as software consultant with a top US company. I belong to Delhi, currently working on H1B visa for over two years. Did Engineering and MBA from Delhi.
Well,I think I am quite sensitive,adpatable, caring and down to earth person with a good sense of humour. Like music(esp. late 70s), travelling and sports.I Strongly believe in Indian values and culture and at the same time very comfortable with western culture. I belong to a very well respected, educated and cultured

Figure 3.1. Virtual Space. Matrimonial advertisement. In Indianmatch.com.

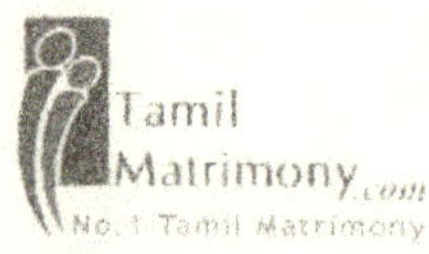

View Profile

Click on **Contact this Profile** option to contact the profile.
Click on **Forward this Profile** option to forward the profile information to a friend or relative.

M197007 - Male

UnMarried looking for UnMarried   **Last Login**: 10-Aug-2003 18:12:21

Name
Krishn...   **Age** : 27

Height . 5 Ft 8 In / 173 Cms

Weight : 65 Kgs / 143 Lbs

Religion : Hindu   **Caste** : Brahmin , Iyer,Tamil,Ashtasahasram

Star : SADAYAM   **Raasi / Moon Sign** : KUMBHA (Aquarius)

Horoscope : Open

Education : Masters - Arts/ Science/ Commerce/ Others

Education in Detail : First Mate(Chief Officer)

Occupation : Merchant Navy - Second Officer (Foreign going)

Hobbies : Interested in Music(Carnatic & English),Reading ,Cricket

Physical Status : Normal

Citizenship : India

Country Living : India

Residing State : Delhi

Description: - Kashyapa Gothram - Ashtasahasram. He has qualified as First Mate (Chief Officer)in Merchant Navy. He is presently serving as Second Officer in a Foreign going vessel.Sails for about 6 months in a year.Life partner can accompany him in ship.He is currently studying to settle for a shore job related to shipping industry in the near future. He is fair; good looking;physical structure in proportion to height; vegetarian;non-smoker; teetotaller; pleasant manners;softspoken;fun loving; goodnatured;caring;adjustable; very much attached to family; gives importance to others' views; religious but open minded.I hail from Tanjore Dist and am presently employed as DGM in IFCI Ltd in Delhi. My wife is home maker.Shriraam's younger brother (Age-22) has completed his graduation (B.E)(ECE)and is recently employed with Reliance Infocomm. Looking for alliance from professionally qualified Iyer brides with minimum graduation qualification ,employed/unemployed, fair and slim between 5'3" and 5'6" tall and age not exceeding 26 years. Sub-sect no bar. Brides with interest in carnatic music are preferred, but not a necessity.

Figure 3.2. Virtual Space. Matrimonial advertisement. In Tamilmatrimony.com.

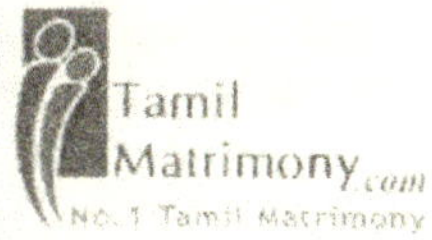

Figure 3.3. Virtual Space. Matrimonial advertisement. In Tamilmatrimony.com.

arrangement is reconstituted because of necessity. The young Indians have modernized the practices allowing the prospective bride and groom a little more than one fleeting meeting and the meetings take place in public venues, quite often decided by the prospective bride and groom without the family encounter. The term which is used now is *assisted arranged marriage*. Thinking back to some friends of mine in India who had gone through the ordeal of meeting the prospective groom, they have narrated how awkward it was to meet the young man along with his mother and several other relatives. She was all dressed to be paraded around like a cattle show, portraying her demure, docile qualities and she hardly spoke to the young man. I remember her saying marriages were not based on love. Today it has moved on to speed-dating, arrangements have become more fluid, though often abiding by the rules and blessings from parents. It is a hybrid situation between the East and the West, holding on to the religion and identity and at the same time reshaping and reconstituting. These arrangements when compared to the earlier meetings is surely a low maintenance and a faster way of finding a mate.

The young people realize, recognize that arranged marriages can well outlast love marriages. They or their mothers first look for compatibility on paper—in which similar education and income levels, religious beliefs, and character outweigh the importance of physical attraction. A prospective bride says, decisions have to be made relatively quickly, often after the second or third meeting, and once you have said yes there is no turning back. Dowries remain common and background still matters too. In speed dating they or their moms look at the CVs and figure out whether they are compatible on paper—right job, right background, right caste. This way, she remarks, the women feel more secure once they are compatible on paper. The compatibility on paper is often decided by checking whether one is of the same caste/religion, like a Tamilian will look for a Tamilian and an engineer will look for an engineer. Parents have accepted these modern approaches and prefer this. At least they can see their children go unwed and they can still claim that it was arranged and he/she can say, "yeah it is arranged but I like her or him."[106]

The examples show how it has changed from the newspaper matrimonial advertisement to the virtual space matrimonial ads; these different ads portray what goes on, what sells, how it sells, the mobile world, the virtual culture, the new media arranged marriages, it just takes three minutes to decide the compatibility . . . and that is why I call it, the death of knowing. Reflecting on these examples and, on the other hand, going back to the start of this section, it is ironic whether it is 3 minutes or 3 years, does one really know the person—the question of compatibility, death of knowing—it is still the death of knowing.

Death of Knowing

Three years
Three minutes
Whose identity
What identity
Are we scrutinizing
Do we know
Can we know
Do they unmoor
Is it unpalatable
Is it compatible
Can One know
Or does the Other remain the OTHER
The Death of knowing

—Rekha Menon

Embracing the Satiate Space

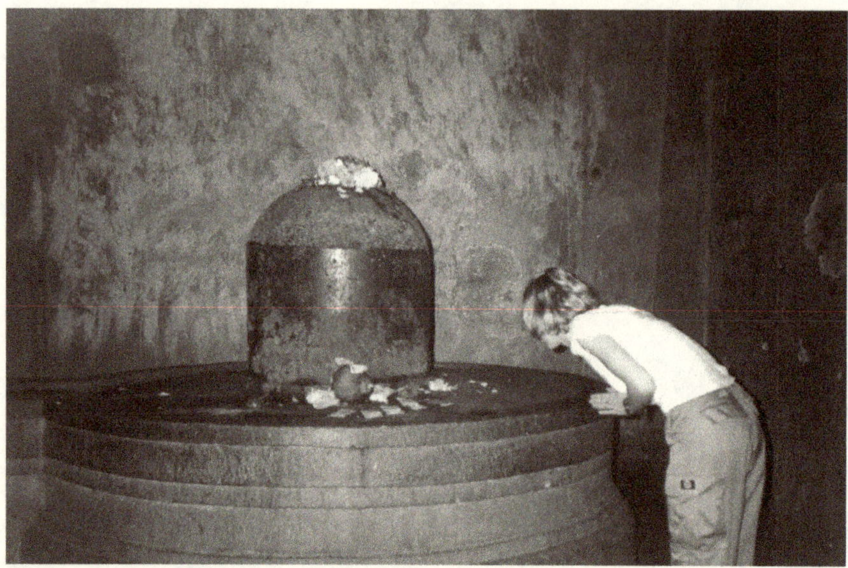

Figure 4.1. The *Ghora, Angrez* (white foreigner) embracing the Sacred Space. Courtesy my friend Monika Brodnicka praying in front of the *Shiva Lingam* in the Hindu temple. Photograph by the author.

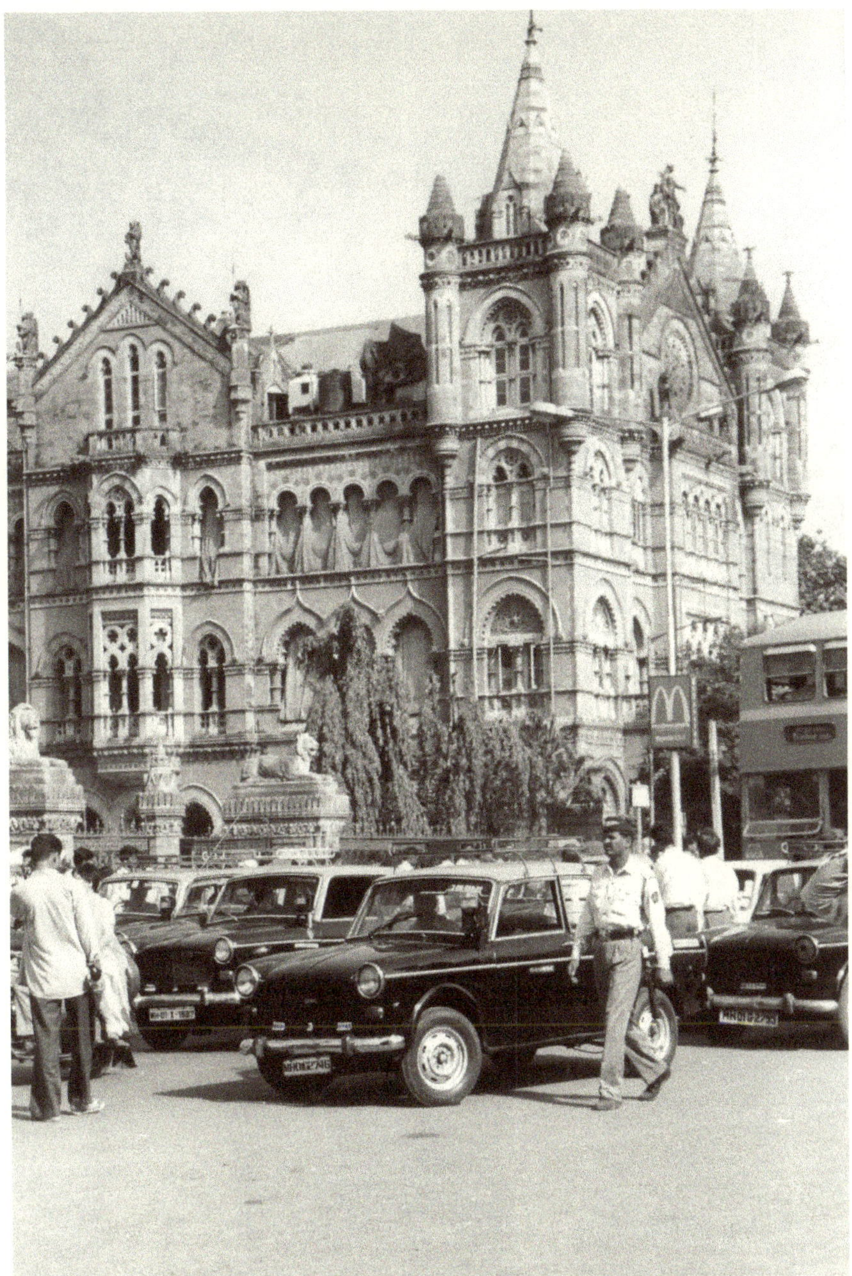

Figure 4.2. Not to miss—the colonized/globalized Space. Alongside the bastardized hybrid Indo-British colonial architecture in Mumbai is the global looming large McDonald (M) arches. Photograph by the author.

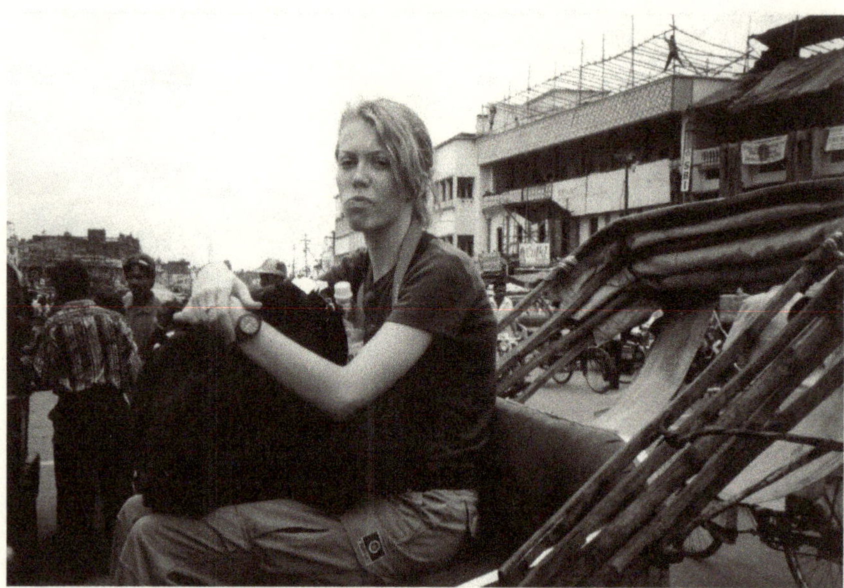

Figure 4.3. The exotic cycle rickshaw ride. The high-techno, globalized crowded cities still boast of cycle rickshaws. Courtesy my friend Monika Brodnicka taking the dicey ride. Photograph by the author.

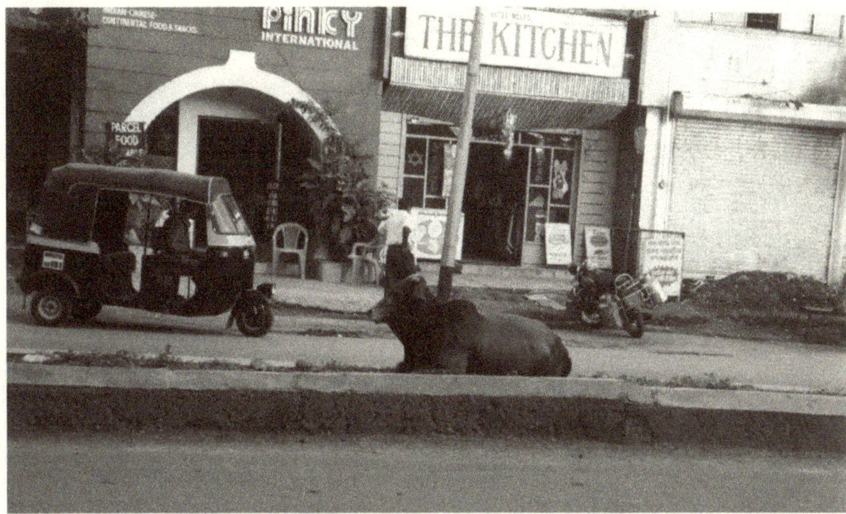

Figure 4.4. In the midst of chaos a sight of leisure. The 'sacred' cow resting in the middle of the road in India unhindered by traffic, noise or pollution. Photograph by the author.

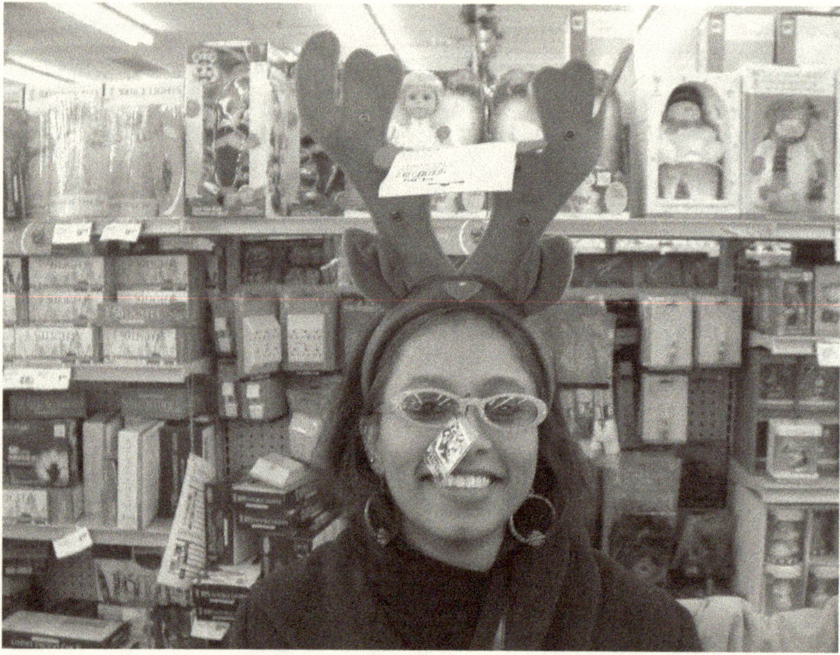

Figure 4.5. Buy all red and green. The excess one gets sucked into during Christmas. Myself in a shop in Boston embracing the red and green stuff. Personal photograph.

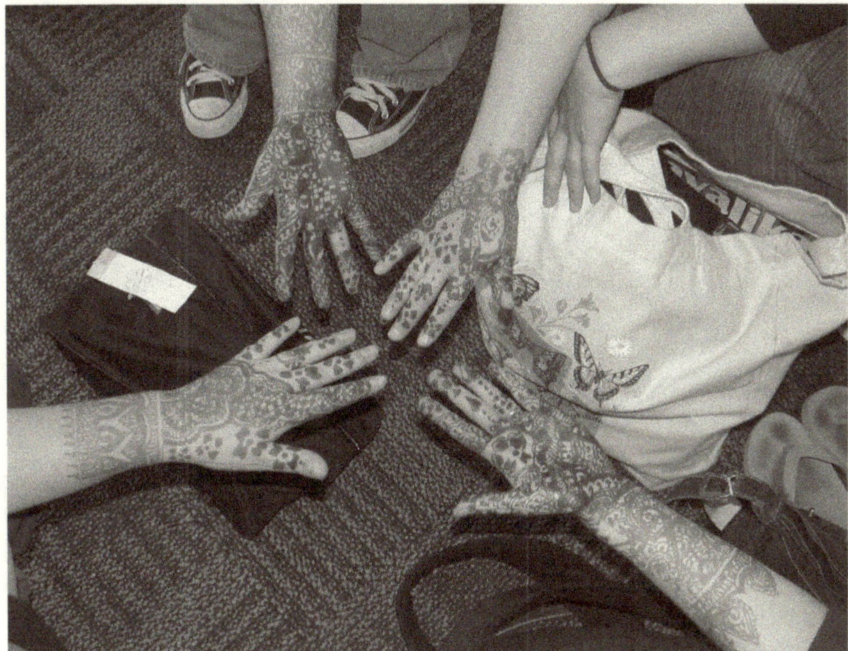

Figure 4.6. Henna mania. When I took my students to India for an on-site art history course, their desire before leaving India was to get their hands and feet adorned with henna and these are the beautiful hands of my students before we left the exotic land. Photograph by the author.

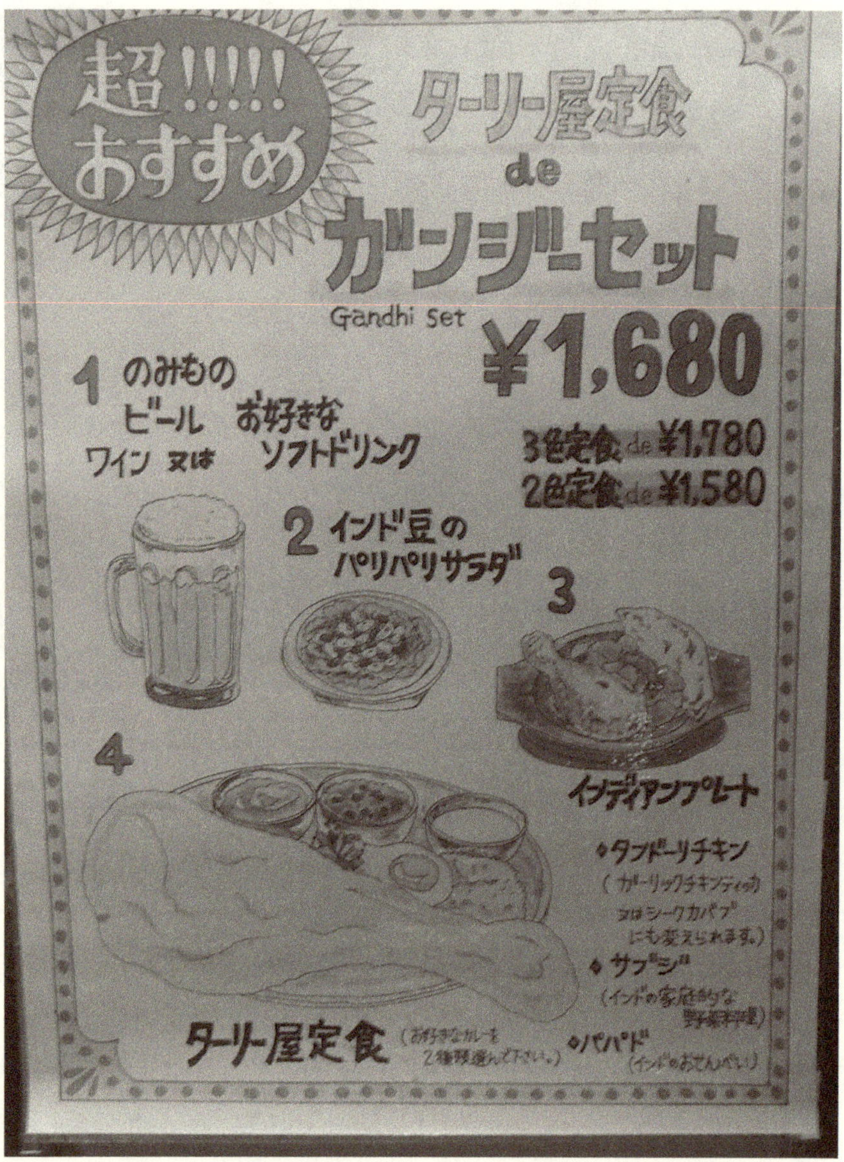

Figure 4.7. Gandhi set—ironic isn't it! When I visited Tokyo, Japan, I found this poster in a restaurant advertising their special meal; *The Gandhi Set*—amusing, don't miss the beer and chicken along with the other sides, they surely have been inspired by Gandhi who preached 'pure' vegetarianism. Photograph by the author.

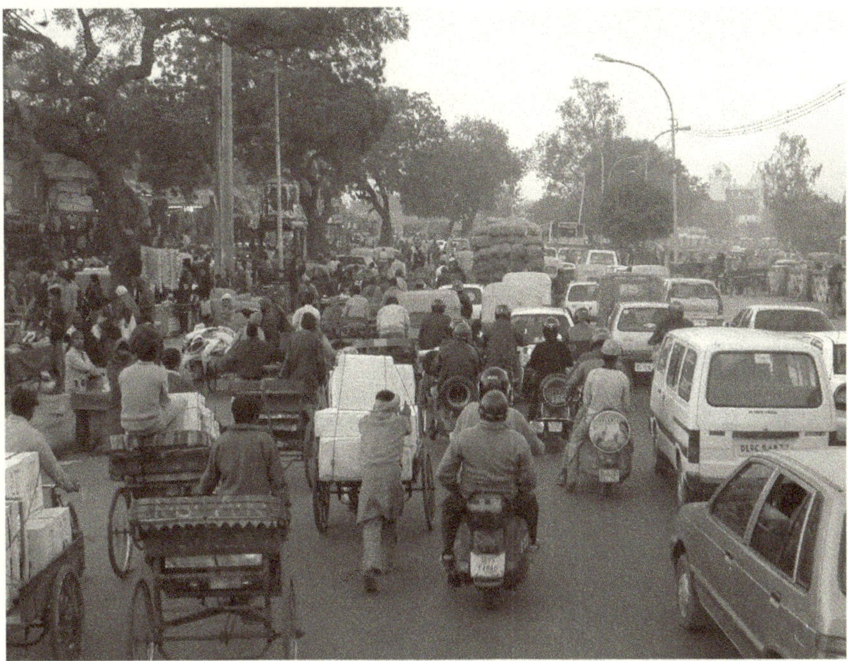

Figure 4.8. Surely India is catching up! One wonders how does one get from place to place—the chaotic traffic in old Delhi. Photograph by the author.

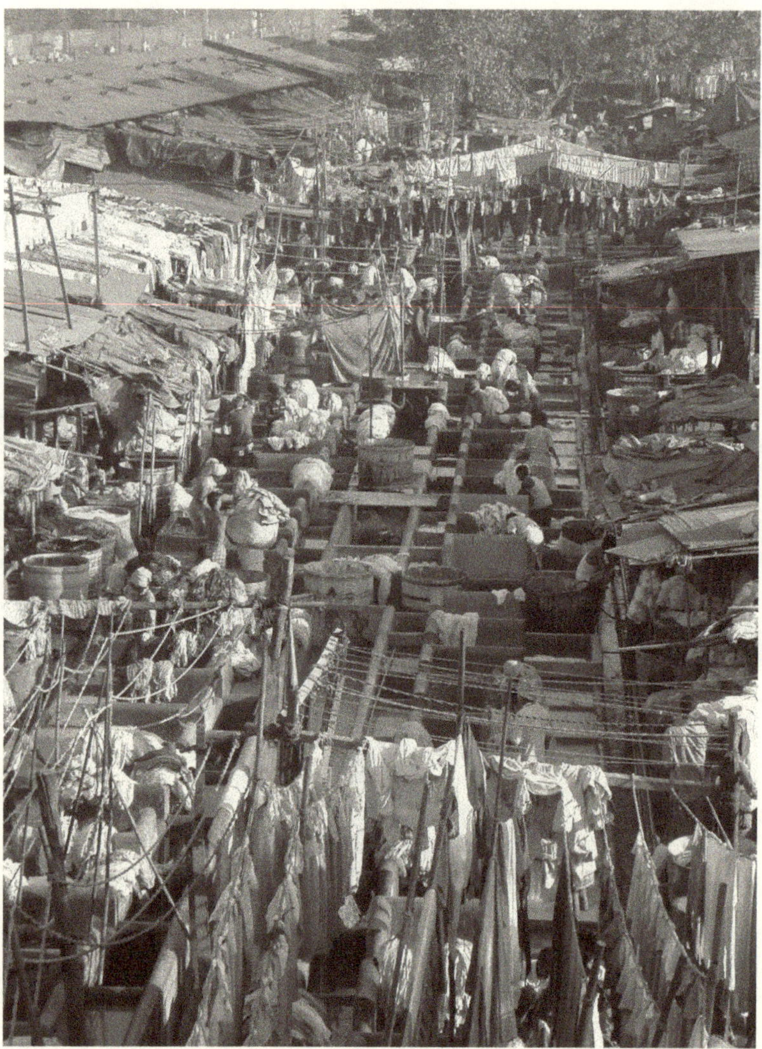

Figure 4.9. Quintessential Indianness—Dhobi Ghat (popular with foreign tourists). The sophisticated dry cleaners (cheap labor)—Dhobi Ghat an integral feature of the city of Mumbai. Dhobis (washerman) collect dirty linen from door to door and return the washed linen in a day or two. The practice that was started by the British Armed Forces (Her Majesty's Army) to have their uniforms washed by the natives still continues in Modern India and is done with such precision. There is no data-base or receipts and still they are returned to the rightful owner hand washed in the open air, sun dried and ironed/pressed, despite the estimated number of clothes washed in a day is around 7.5 lakhs. Photograph by the author.

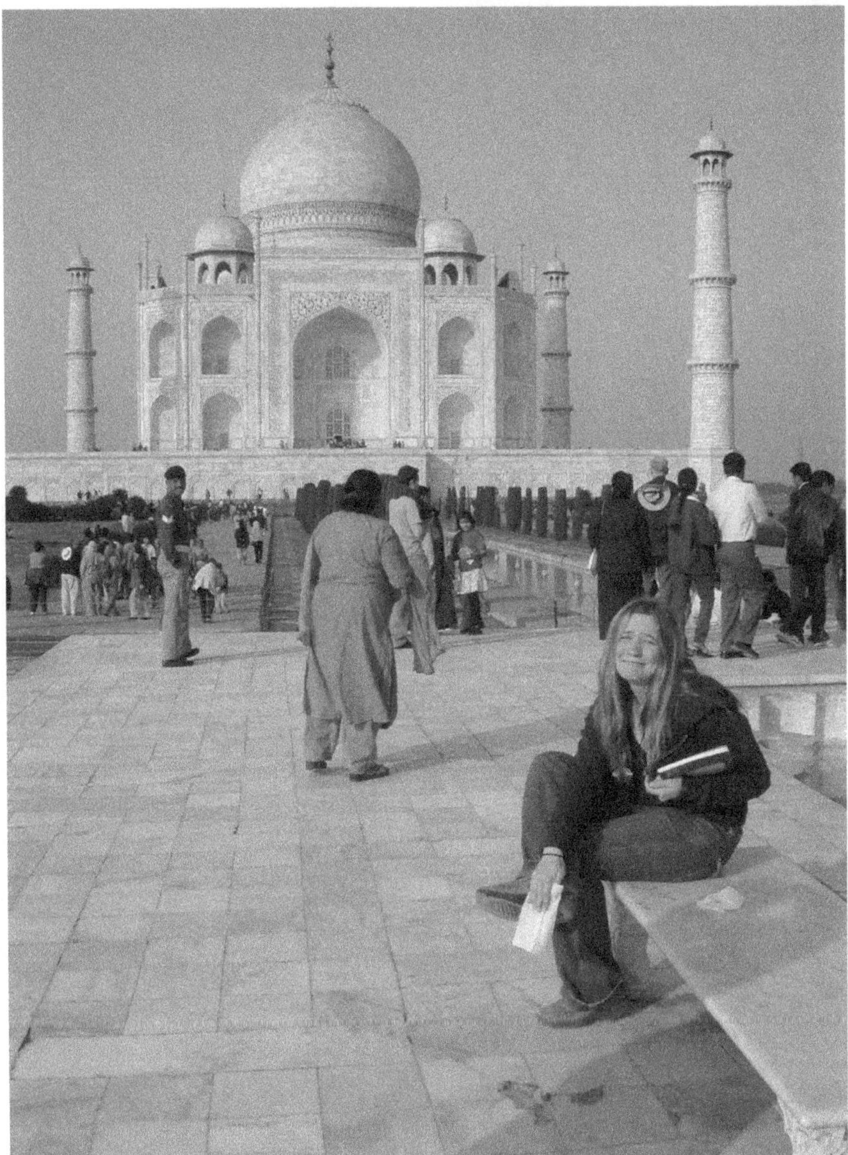

Figure 4.10. The glorious Taj. Who would imagine while standing in front of the most beautiful monument, basking in its glory, admiring one of the wonders of the world, one would step on fecal matter. Courtesy Anneliese Gryta, who was my student, who accidentally stepped on fecal matter while admiring the glorious Taj Mahal. Photograph by the author.

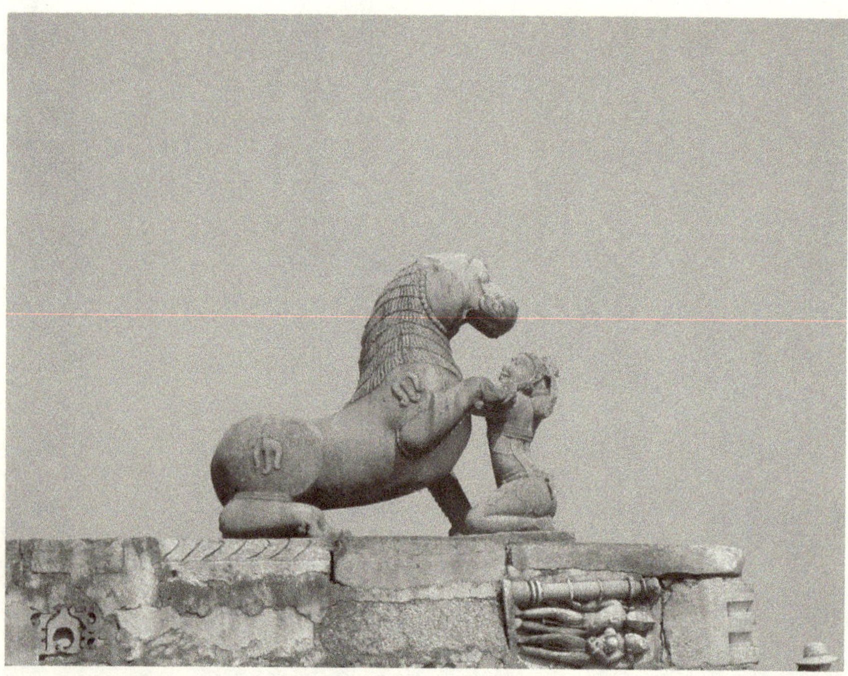

Figure 4.11. The beautiful embrace. The sculpture from Khajuraho—surely embracing the Satiate Space. Photograph by the author.

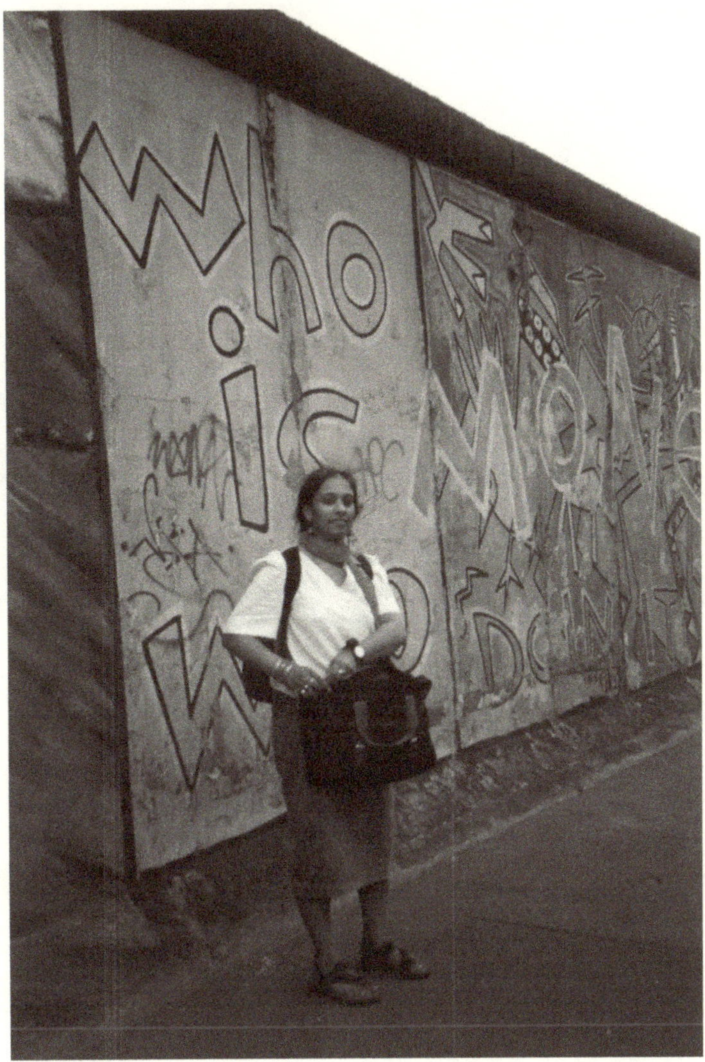

Figure 4.12. Who is who—neither here nor there. Standing in front of what is left of the Berlin Wall, I thought to myself, Who Am I—Do I Really Know. Personal photograph.

Afterword

Liberated or Trapped: Third World's Third World Dreamings

> Looking into the mirror, the Black woman or I asked, "Mirror, Mirror, on the wall, who's the fairest of them all?" The Mirror answered, Snow White, you Black bitch, and don't you forget it!" not anymore. . . .
>
> Today the Mirror answers, Don't you know, YOU BITCH . . . the Exotic One

These telling words inscribe how being a Black/brown woman from the Third World, an African, or Asian . . . how did the standard change . . . where they were always excluded as we don't have the porcelain skin, long silken blonde hair, delicate features, the norm of Western beauty when compared to what they called us, the much maligned unattractive, monstrous, grotesque women of color who were deplorable and detested . . . now how come the mirror answers the fairest is not the Snow White but the exotic. Are we the fairest, are we the beautiful exotic, liberated . . . or are we really trapped? . . .

In a global world, where one commodifies desires and to its end the desirous objects, the desire and identity become ambiguous. Ethnic identity becomes camouflaged by global desire and we get colonized, sucked into the Global Space. Is this space, a fallacy of identity, are we victimized or thriving, how do we create identities? The aesthetics of globalization, the irony of the seduction, the lived experience of the nostalgic dreamings. Are we the Third World-liberated or trapped in the idiom, desirous of the global?

The other day my colleague tells me accusingly how lucky I am, being an Indian, India today is prospering, they are taking all the jobs . . . our jobs . . . what with all this outsourcing . . . at that moment I wanted to say, "why not, it is high time India gains." What with all the exploitation that has been happening, from the time of the British and by the United States later, intellectually exploiting and colonizing us materially . . . so why not let India enjoy it for some time we deserve it . . . are we really gaining? Isn't it another kind of exploitation, cheap labor just as before only it is more sophisticated? The outsourcing basically is getting an Indian to do the work at a lesser price when compared to someone doing it in the United States. So, are we really gaining, are we becoming prosperous or isn't it another form of cheap exploitation? . . . Nevertheless don't get me wrong, I enjoy the space, I am in the United States, for me, an alien it is still a *Seductive Space*.

When people say you are taking our jobs and the media has been splashing reports of American workers losing jobs as a result of work being exported overseas . . . and I imagine for a moment . . . **WANT YOU TO IMAGINE** . . . **Self Deportation**, inspired by Guillermo Gomez-Pena taken from *Dangerous Border Crossers*, "The Self Deportation Project, 1995." (I have changed the version to imagine/fit my Indian milieu).

I imagine New York city, a city full of immigrants, Indians, people of color, aliens, as we are called. . . . You perceive yourself as an "angry White male," with your beautiful Indian wife and two hybrid kids. Today, what a day, I have to go to work . . . plenty to do, have to finish lot of Lenox-related projects with the help of my Indian friend, Sam alias Shamasundaram, just cannot get his name right . . . oh shit . . . have to fill gas and I am not looking forward to the long drive from New Jersey. I stop for gas, but the gas station is closed. What's happened, where are the Indians who pump gas. I don't know that all the attendants went back to India. I try to call a cab, my favorite cab driver, Santa Singh or may be I will try Banta Singh, you know my wife says Sardars are so reliable; but there are no cabs because mainly the Indians quit the day before. Somehow I have to get to the office to find Samy boy to finish the project. Surprised my American colleagues are watching TV as the Indian engineers have quit so they don't know what to do next . . . and they are watching the TV in total disbelief. A nervous President Bush is pleading for all unemployed Indians, Anglos and Africans, African-Americans to show up immediately to the closest emergency labor recruitment center, we will offer HI-B work permits. The country is paralyzed. The disappeared Indian and labor force must be replaced overnight.

At lunch time, I discover that most restaurants are closed; I try to get to the convenience store run by a Patel, who has a motel too close by, to get a snack. It was closed and the hotel across was also closed, oops the Indians who clean up, who wait on you have left, and the banks are going crazy. All across the country, millions of Indians with their suitcases in hand are lining up at the bank counters to withdraw their accounts on their way back to their homelands. I decided to go home, as I remembered I had an appointment, to take my kid to the Indian doctor. Walking of course to the train station, because my car was parked somewhere on the other side of town and I noticed and smelled the stench, the dumpsters are overflowing as the garbage pickers, immigrants—they have not done their rounds being the day of the week when garbage is picked up. I reach home, my Indian wife is devastated as most of her relatives have chosen to go back home, to their old country. She is also furious because the babysitter, Maria, did not show up. She explains she had to stay home to take care of the kids and missed all her work appointments. She even had to take the kids for shopping, which Maria normally does. They stood in an eternal line in the supermarket, only to find that the long line was because there was only one counter open. The supermarket manager explained and apologized, he said that the Indian workers did not show up today. We decide to go see the doctor and oh dear the clinic is closed/shut down as the Indian doctor quit this morning to go back to India. Perplexed I go to bed, only to wake up from a nightmare. I was toiling away carrying a heavy load under the scorching sun . . . was I part of building the railways? . . .

Next morning I turn on the TV. A panicked President delivers the bad news: very few responded to his desperate call for workers. The unemployed citizens were clearly not inspired by the ideas of working for minimum wage and no benefits. The nation's construction, the fast pace software industries are all in disarray. New York city has declared bankruptcy. . . . Luckily, India has offered to send some Indians, emergency workers, cleaners, engineers, doctors to clear the mess. Desperate President Bush proceeds to beg the remaining Indians to stay back. Now I cool down. Its been a hard day . . . I sip my delicious tea from Darjelling, India and turn up my favorite fusion Indian hip-hop Banghra . . . and I can smell the aroma of the spicy hot *vindaloo* . . . and maybe today I will watch the movie *Guru*, it might inspire me to meditate and do yoga . . . that was the self deportation project . . . I imagined. . . .

With all this discussion, this imagination, one can still say that the creation of the Other can also be a reversal. As Fanon observes, "Europe is literally the creation of the Third world, so is the Other a creation of the Self."[107] The pressure for decolonization is as old as European colonialism itself. Sometimes, by using colonialism as a platform to say that the Other is the victimized, I am reminded of Sartre's announcement, "the settler which is in every one of us is being savagely rooted out. Let us look at ourselves, if we can bear to, and see what is becoming of us. . . ." Can we see our naked selves today or are we all so caught up in this fold of western logic, thus calling ourselves the Other, the victimized by the colonizer. Is it possible for us to get rid of all these hermenuetics and be who we are or do we know who we are?

How Many FOOTSTEPS. . . .

The stage black black now . . .
Out of that soft, dirty, belly, swollen with fat----------------
I came out

There and I ask myself
and I ask
and I ask
and I ask
               I say:
What is my name
   What is my name
               What is my name
                       What is my name. . . .
But the dark line on this stranger's belly cried out to me: **You can't get away from me**
What is your name darling
     "   angel
     "   honey
     "   baby

BABY—You can't get away from me, I' m the one who formed you, your body and
     your spirit, with my flesh and blood ---- you're mine, all mine
MINE   The **WHITE FATHERS** told us. . . .
"I THINK, THEREFORE, I AM"   and the   **BLACK MOTHER** within each of
     us --- the poet---whispers in
our dreams ----*I feel therefore I can be free*. . . .
AS IF
To move leaping from occupying space to occupying the idea the thought to make it
     your own
Time and again these resources impelling how to flee, run from subvert
we forcing we to live in them
Its not worth it
and *I would ask What's not worth it*
Your name is that of a condemned MAN
YOU have no NAME
WE don't want you, UNCLEAN lying there in vomit filth
Between the legs   the space
within the womb   the space
colonized like place and space   **around her**
defend me from them that rise up against me. Deliver me from the workers of inequity and
     save me from **bloody men.**
To protect the space that lies. . . .   this dis   place
must not be sold
must not be given away
BEWARE
Along comes the **WhiteButts** to embarrass our people to wear corsets and
     girdles around our throats   Those **ENGLISH** and those damn wigs—
     What is it with people who need to conquer people?
Bitch take it like a man
                    I   *yelled*

Say it Say it Bitch

(How I wish this would all end How I WISH i could walk free in this world And could find my life again)

Tooo much has happened   For toooo Long
We insects, have learned how to see in the dark

Do you realize its tooo late, that I will never be grateful to you
I had fought as best I COULD against mother's bowels, which were pushing me imperiously
down a slippery slope that would lead to the brink of the void, to this borrowed life . . .

The in-betweeners **remember**
The first question How was your day today----------------
the common language   between   the how   and much fail
the **go away** is sure to kick in

and to keep my cursed tongue locked up behind my teeth.
I knew what should and should not be said
I became aware of my situation. Sublimation was impossible

We don't
we don't
we don't give a damn
we don't give a shit
we won't give an inch   **not for you   or you   or you**
One needs a place to begin
A place from which to build

We live in a space tormented space between sanctity and damnation
Desolation and despair are only a breath away
in release of that emotion; in hearing the rage and frustration
nonetheless; an intensity that will be multiplied

An evil voice will scream
                    he can hear yoooooo
                                        he can hear yooooooooooooooooooooooooo
I can hear you

I don't know how long I can go on like this
Light out
light out
light out
light out
light out
My God Time --- it it is it late   passes   was that me again
LIGHT OUT
So slowly I just think

Is it really time to GO
TO GO
STOP GO   STOP GO   STOP GO
STOP   **STOP**   **STOP**
STOP IT
SHIT
  SHIT
    SHIT
THIS IS WEIRD. Today is the second day at home and, as usual, I can't figure out
WHO I am
I Stop I Walk, I Stop   **OTHERS Walk**

—Rekha Menon

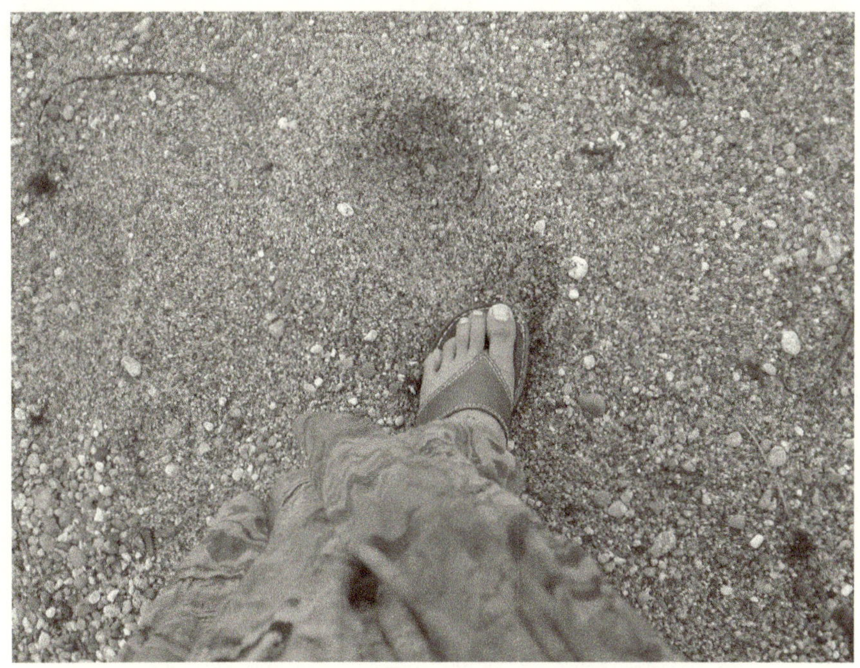

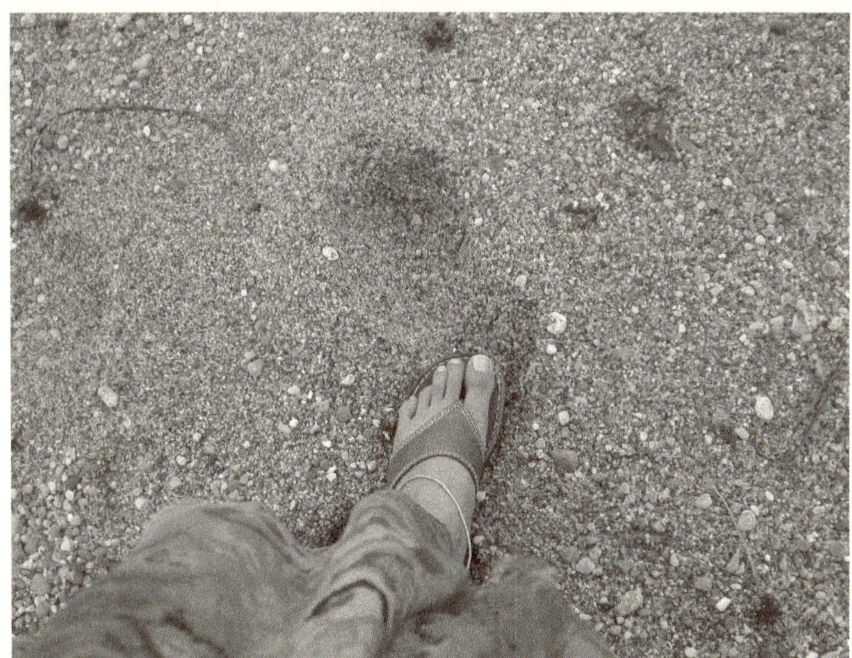

How Many FOOTSTEPS. . . . Photographs by the author.

Notes

1. Gloria Anzaldua, "Speaking in Tongues: A Letter to 3rd World Women Writers," *This Bridge*, 1996, p. 166.

2. Trinh T. Minh-ha, *Women Native Other* (Bloomington: Indiana University Press, 1989), p. 38. Inspired by Minh-ha's writing, from the section *"Write Your Body,"* taken from her book.

3. Nirmal Verma, "India and Europe—Some Reflections on Self and Other," *Between Tradition and Modernity: India's Search for Identity*, ed. Fred Dallmayr & G. N. Devy (Walnut Creek, London & New Delhi: Altamira Press, 1998), p. 332. This article is a text of a lecture delivered at the University of Heidelberg, Germany, and is taken from the journal, *Kavita Asia*, 121–144.

4. Verma, 333.

5. Verma, 333.

6. Verma, 336.

7. Verma, 336.

8. Verma, 335 (Verma, quotes Nirad Chaudhuri's observations).

9. Verma, 337.

10. Verma, 338.

11. Verma, 339.

12. Verma, 342.

13. Verma, 343.

14. Verma, 344.

15. Verma, 345.

16. Verma, 346.

17. Verma, 346.

18. Verma, 352.

19. Jacques Derrida, "White Mythology" (1971), *Margins of Philosophy*, trans. Alan Bass (Chicago: Chicago University Press, 1982), p. 213.

20. Robert Young, *White Mythologies, Writing History and the West* (London & New York: Routledge, 1990), p. 9.

21. Levinas' account of the role of theory as vision, and its claim in Plato to a disinterested contemplation of being is discussed in detail by Derrida, "Violence and Metaphysics. An Essay on Thought of Emmanuel Levinas," *Writing and Difference*, trans. Alan Bass (London: Routledge & Keagan Paul, 1978), pp. 84–92.

22. Michel Foucault, "Politics and the Study of Discourse," *Ideology and Consciousness* 3 (1978), 24.

23. M. Nourbese Philip, *A Genealogy of Resistance* (Canada: The Mercury Press, 1997), p. 94. Inspired by Philip's writing, the line, "Between the legs The Space" is taken from her book.

24. Algis Mickunas, "The Cosmic Traces." Unpublished article, presented at the Husserl Circle Conference, Ohio University.

25. Choodamani Nandagopal, "Dancing for the Gods," *Hindu Folio* (an Indian Newspaper), Sunday, December 1997, p. 18.

26. Nandagopal, 18.

27. Nandagopal, 18.

28. Nandagopal, 19.

29. Mohan Khokar, "The Renaissance of Indian Dance and its Consequences," *Dances of India*, Vivekananda Kendra Patrika, Vol. 10, No. 2 (Madras: Vivekananda Kendra, 1981), 13.

30. Khokar, 13.

31. Jennifer Dunning, "A Celebration of the Spiritual Where Some See Sin," *New York Times*, November 15. 1998, p. 12.

32. Devara Dasimayya, trans. A. K. Ramanujan.

33. Dunning, 12.

34. Rustom Bharucha, *Chandralekha Woman Dance Resistance* (India: Harper Collins, 1995) p. 157.

35. Barucha, p. 170.

36. Barucha, pp. 182–183.

37. Nanda Tanmaya Kumar, "The Masala Bhangra Girl," *India Abroad*, July 19, 2002.

38. Alexander Cunningham, *Archaeological Survey of India*, Vol. 2, 1862–1865.

39. Susie Tharu and K. Lalita, eds., *Women Writing in India 600 B.C. to the Present Vol. 1* (New York: The Feminist Press, 1991), pp. 1–3.

40. Tharu and Lalita, 1–3.

41. Tharu and Lalita, 3.

42. Tharu and Lalita, 5.

43. W. Frazer, "Letter to the Chief Secretary," Fort William (now Madras), 25. 9. 1828. H. Sharp, *Selections from Educational Records*, Vol. 1 (Calcutta: Superintendent, Govt. Printing, India, 1923), p. 13.

44. Minutes of J. Farish, 28. 8. 1938. Quoted in B. K. Boman-Behram, *Educational Controversies of India: The Cultural Conquest of India under British Imperialism* (Bombay: Taraporevala Sona and Co., 1942), p. 239.

45. Katherine Mayo, *Mother India* (New York: Blue Ribbon Books, 1927). Mayo was an American journalist whose text permeated with overtly racist terms and analyses.

46. Amachya Deshachi Sthiti (Nagpur, 1937), pp. 17–19. (Chandra quotes Chiplunkar.)

47. Sudhir Chandra, *The Oppressive Present* (New York: Oxford University Press, 1992), pp. 17–20.

48. Amachya Deshachi Sthiti, p. 20. (Chandra quotes Chiplunkar.)

49. Wendy Chapkis, "Skin Deep," in *Beauty Secrets: Women and Politics of Beauty* (Boston: South End Press, 1994), pp. 37–38.

50. Chapkis, p. 39 (Saatchi and Saatchi Annual Report, 1982, 15).

51. Chapkis, p. 39.

52. Christopher Pinney, "Moral Topophilia: The Significations of Landscape in Indian Oleographs," *The Anthropology of Landscape Perspectives on Place and Space,* eds. E. Hirsch and M. O'Hanlon (Oxford, New York: Oxford University Press, 1995), p. 83.

53. Lynda Nead, *Chila Kumari Burman: Beyond Two Cultures* (London: Kala Press, 1995), p. 67.

54. Nead, 64.

55. Nead, 70.

56. Gary Hesse, *Contact Sheet, Alien* (Syracuse, NY: Light Work, 2002), p. 2.

57. Hesse, 2.

58. Interview with Deepa Mehta on Rediff, *On the Net, Movies: An Interview with Deepa Mehta,* Suparn Verma; www.redfindia.com/entair/oct/24.htm.

59. The Hindu fundamentalists, leaders of the Shiv Sena and their cronies in Delhi and Bombay were opposed to the film for its depiction of a lesbian relationship and attacked and prevented the film from running, particularly in Bombay.

60. Parvez Sharma, "Burning down the House," *Trikone Magazine* (April, 1999), 8. Sharma looks at the turmoil in India over Mehta's film and reports on what the intelligentsia and not-so-intelligent-sia are saying about the film.

61. Jyoti Puri, *Body Desire in Post-colonial India* (New York: Routledge, 1999), p. 206.

62. *Fishers of Men,* Documentary film, directed by Ranjan Kamath and Padmavathi Rao (Madhya Pradesh, India, 1997). This program is organized by the Hindu fundamentalists such as the Rashitriya Swayamsevak Sangh and the Vishwa Hindu Parishad.

63. Algis Mickunas, "Cultural Logics and the Search for National Identities," *Phenomenology of the Cultural Disciplines* (Netherlands: Kluwer, 1993), pp. 147–170.

64. Gomez-Pena Guillermo, *Warriors for Gringostroika* (St Paul: Graywolf Press, 1993), pp. 43–44.

65. Trinh T. Minh-ha, *Woman, Native, Other* (Bloomington: Indiana University Press, 1989), p. 98.

66. Gloria Anzaldua, *Borderlands/La Frontera* (San Francisco: Spinsters/Aunt Lute Press, 1987), p. 3.

67. Victoria Ebin, *The Body Decorated* (New York: Thames and Hudson, 1979), p. 5.

68. Salah M. Hassan, "Henna Mania: Body Painting as a Fashion Statement, from Tradition to Madonna," *The Art of African Fashion* (Eritrea: Africa World Press, 1998).

69. Hassan, 104.

70. Hassan, 110.

71. Hassan, 114.

72. Hassan, 106.

73. Hassan, 122.

74. Jon Pareles articulates this in the *New York Times* (June 21, 1998).

75. Sherry Chopra (Editorial *Ottawa Citizen*, September 30, 1998), also mentioned by Hassan on p. 124.

76. Chopra, September 30, 1998.

77. bell hooks, *Black Looks, Race and Representation* (Boston: South End Press, 1992), p. 157 (also mentioned by Hassan on p. 116).

78. Geoffrey Moorehouse, *Calcutta* (Harmondsworth, 1974).

79. Alexander Cunningham, *Archaeological Survey of India* (Report of the Year 1862–65, Vol. 11).

80. J. R. Ackerley, *Hindoo Holiday: An Indian Journal* (1932), pp. 23–24. Also mentioned by Benita Parry, *Delusions and Discoveries* (London, New York: Verso, 1998), p. 31.

81. Parry, 31.

82. Kobena Mercer, *Welcome to the Jungle* (New York & London: Routledge, 1994), p. 176. Mercer quotes Bhabha.

83. Hassan, 126–127.

84. Fred Pfeil, "No Basta Teorizar: In-Difference to Solidarity in Contemporary Fiction, Theory and Practice," *Scattered Hegemonies: Postmodernity and Transnational Feminist Practices*, Eds., Inderpal Grewal and Caren Kaplan (Minneapolis: University of Minnesota Press, 1994), pp. 222–223.

85. Shakuntala Banaji, "Private Lives and Public Spaces: The Precarious Pleasures of Gender Discourse. In *Raja Hindustani, Women a Cultural Review Open Forum* Vol. 13, Summer (2002), 179.

86. Amitava Kumar, *Bombay London New York* (Routledge: New York London, 2002), p. 216.

87. Kumar, p. 217.

88. Giti Thadani, *Sakhiyani* (London, New York: Caassell, 1996), p. 5.

89. Thadani, p. 68.

90. Thadani, p. 68.

91. Vivekananda, *Complete Works* Vol. 2 (Calcutta, 1963), p. 476.

92. Thadani, 68–69.

93. Yasmin Tambiah, "Decolonization and Third World Lesbian Identities." Unpublished paper presented at the Seminar on the History of Alternative Sexualities, New Delhi (1993).

94. Vivekananda, 506.

95. *The Laws of Manu*, trans. Buhler Muller (Delhi: Motilal Banarasidas, 1964).

96. Suruchi Thapar, "Woman as Activists; Woman as Symbols: A Study of the Indian Nationalist Movement," *Feminist Review* No. 44, Summer (1993), 87.

97. Thapar, 87.

98. Gandhi, *The Collected Works of Mahatma Gandhi* Vol. xiiii (Ahmedabad: Navajivan, 1971), p. 12.

99. Sucheta Mazumdar, "Moving Away from a Secular Vision? Women, Nation and Cultural Construction of Hindu India," *Identity Politics and Woman: Cultural Reassertions and Feminisms in International Perspective*, ed., Valentine M. Moghadam (Boulder, CO: Westerview Press, 1994), p. 257.

100. Partha Chatterjee, "The Nationalist Resolution of the Woman's Question," *Recasting Woman: Essays in Indian Colonial History*, ed., Kumkum Sangari and Suresh Vaid (New Brunswick, NJ: Rutgers University Press, 1990), pp. 239–243.

101. Thadani, 70.

102. Sudhir Kakar, *The Inner World* (Delhi, 1978), p. 35.

103. Chris Berry, Fran Martin, and Audrey Yue, eds., *Mobile Culture* (Durham & London: Duke University Press, 2003), p. 1.

104. Berry, Martin and Yue, 2.

105. Berry, Martin and Yue, 2.

106. Notes taken from the following articles: Alvarez, Lizette, "Arranged Marriages, Rearranged Asian Britons Nudge Out Matchmakers," *International Herald Tribune*, June 23, 2003; and also from *India Abroad*, July 27, 2001 and from Virtual Space on "Speed Dating."

107. Frantz Fanon, *The Wretched of the Earth*, trans. Constance Farrington (Harmondsworth: Penguin, 1967), p. 81.

Artwork by the Author
(The artwork is a dialogue, I portray myself caught in the midst of the in-between Seductive Space, which I love.)
Cover Page—Gentlemen Prefer Indian Exotic
p. 10—Dress Me Up
p. 40—Can You Speak English
p. 58—Tales of the Indian Exotic Bitch
Last Page—Goodbye to India

Bibliography

Ackerley, J. R. (1932). *Hindoo Holiday: An Indian Journal*. New York: Viking Press.

Alvarez, Lizette. (2003, June 23). Arranged marriages, rearranged Asian Britons nudge out matchmakers. *International Herald Tribune*

Anand, Mulk Raj. (1960). *Kama Kala*. Geneva: Nagel Publishers.

Anand, Keval Krishna. (1982). *Indian philosophy: The concept of Karma*. Delhi: Bharatiya Vidya Prakasham.

Anantharangachar, N. S. (1967). *The philosophy of Sadhana*. Mysore: University of Mysore.

AnnMilford-Lutzker, Mary. (1999). Intersections: Urban and village art in India. *Art Journal.*

Anzaldua, Gloria. (1987). *Borderlands/La frontera*. San Francisco: Spinsters/Aunt Lute Press.

Anzaldua, Gloria. (1996). "Speaking in Tongues: A Letter to 3rd World Women Writers." *This Bridge*, 166.

Appadurai, Angadipuram. (1971). *Political ideas in modern India: Impact of the west*. Bombay: Academic Books.

Appadurai, Arjun. (1996). *Modernity at large: Cultural dimensions of globalization*. Minneapolis: University of Minnesota Press.

Apparao, Sharan. (1997). The aesthetics of art. *Hindu Folio* [Indian Newspaper]. In Hindu.

Ashcroft, Bill Griffiths, & Gareth Tiffin, Helen. (1995). *The post-colonial reader*. London, New York: Routledge.

Banaji, Shakuntala. (2002). Private Lives and Public Spaces; The Precarious Pleasures of Gender Discourse. In *Raja Hindustani, Women a Cultural Review Open Forum, 13*, 179.

Belvalkar, S. K., & Ranade. (1972). *History of Indian philosophy* (Vol. 1 and Vol. 2). New Delhi: Oriental Books.

Berry, Chris, Martin, Fran, & Yue, Audrey. (2003). *Mobile cultures*. Durham & London: Duke University Press.

Bhabha, Homi. (1983a). Difference, discrimination and the discourse of colonialism. In Francis Baker (Ed.), *The politics of theory*. Colchester, UK: University of Essex.

Bhabha, Homi. (1983b). The other question. *Screen,* 24(6).

Bhabha, Homi. (1994). *The location of culture.* London and New York: Routledge.

Bharucha, Rustom. (1995). *Chandralekha Woman dance resistance.* India: Harper Collins.

Bhattacharya, Narenderanath. (1982). *History of Tantric religion.* New Delhi: Manohar.

Boman-Behram, B.K. (1942), *Educational Controversies of India: The Cultural Conquest of India under British Imperialism.* Bombay: Taraporevala Sona and Co.

Brand, Dionne. (1999). *At the fall and change of the Moon.* New York: Grove Press.

Bryson, Norman. (1983). *Vision and painting.* London: The Macmillan Press.

Butler, Judith. (1991). The imperialist subject. *Journal of Urban and Cultural Studies,* 2(1).

Butler, Judith. (1993). *Bodies that matter.* New York & London: Routledge.

Chandra, Sudhir. (1992). *The oppressive present.* Oxford: New York University Press.

Chapkis, Wendy. (1994). Skin deep. In *Beauty secrets: Women and politics of beauty.* Boston: South End Press.

Chatterjee, Partha. (1986). *Nationalist thought and the colonial world: A derivative discourse.* London: Zed Books.

Chatterjee, Partha. (1990). The nationalist resolution of the woman's question. In Kumkum Sangari & Suresh Vaid (Eds.), *Recasting woman: Essays in Indian colonial history.* New Brunswick, NJ: Rutgers University Press.

Chopra, Sherry. (1998, September 30). Editorial. *Ottawa Citizen.*

Coomaraswamy, Ananda Kentish. (1934). *The transformation of nature in art.* New York: Dover Publications.

Coomaraswamy, Ananda Kentish. (1947). *Time and eternity.* Ascona, Switzerland: Artibus Asia.

Cunningham, Alexander. (1862–65). *Archaecological survey of India* (Vol. II). New Delhi.

Deleuze, Gilles, & Guttari, Felix. (1983). *Anti Oedipus capitalism and schizophrenia.* Minneapolis: University of Minnesota Press.

Derrida, Jacques. (1971). White mythology. In *Margins of philosophy* (Alan Bass, Trans.). Chicago: Chicago University Press.

Derrida, Jacques. (1978). Violence and metaphysics. In *Writing and Difference* (Alan Bass, Trans.). London: Routledge & Kegan Paul.

Divakaruni, Banerjee Chitra. (1995). *Arranged marriage.* New York: Anchor Books.

Dunning, J. (1998, November). *New York Times.*

Dutt, Nirupama. (1999, July 4). Will the west be won. Review on the show Traditions and Tensions., *The Express Magazine.*

Eagleton, Terry. (1999). In the gaudy supermarket. *London Review of Books,* 21(10).

Ebin, Victoria. (1979). *The body decorated.* New York: Thames and Hudson.

Exit Art, Gallery Brochure. (1992). The Hybrid State Exhibit.

Fanon, Frantz. (1965). *A dying colonialism* (Haakon Chevalier, Trans.). New York: Grove Press.

Fanon, Frantz. (1967a). *Black skin white masks*. New York: Grove Press.

Fanon, Frantz. (1967b). *The wretched of the earth* (Constance Farrington, Trans.). Harmondsworth: Penguin.

Featherstone, Mike (Ed.). (1990). *Global culture. Nationalism, globalization and modernity*. London, Newbury Park, CA: Sage.

Featherstone Mike, Scott Lash, & Roland Robertson (Eds.). (1995). *Global modernities*. London, Thousand Oaks, CA: Sage.

Fisher, Jean. (1995). *Global visions: Towards a new internationalism in the visual arts*. London: Kala Press.

Fishers of Men (1997). India, Documentary film (Ranjan Kamath & Padmavathi Rao, Dir.).

Foucault, Michel. (1978). Politics and the study of discourse. In *Ideology and consciousness. History Workshop Journal*.

Foucault, Michel. (1990). *The history of sexuality* (Robert Hurley, Trans.). New York: Vintage.

Frazer, W., Letter to the Chief Secretary, Fort William (now Madras), 25.9.1828.

Gandhi. (1971). *The collected works of Mahatma Gandhi* (Vol. 43). Ahmedabad: Navajivan.

Gedalof, Irene. (1999). *Against purity*. London, New York: Routledge.

Goodchild, Philip. (1996). *Deleuze and Guattari: An introduction to the politics of desire*. London; Thousand Oaks, CA: Sage.

Goldberg, Theo David. (1990). *Anatomy of racism*. Minneapolis: University of Minnesota Press.

Grosz, Elizabeth. (1994). *Volatile bodies*. Bloomington, Indianapolis: Indiana University Press.

Guarnizo, Luis E., & Michael, P. Smith (Eds.). (1998). *Transnationalism from below*. New Brunswick, London: Transaction Books.

Guillermo, Gomez-Pena. (1993). *Warriors for Gringostroika*. St. Paul: Graywolf Press.

Guillermo, Gomez-Pena. (2000). *Dangerous border crossers*. London: Routledge.

Hahn, Kimiko. (1999). *Volatile*. New York: Hanging Loose Press.

Hahn, Kimiko, & Mura, David (Eds.). (1997). *The Asian Pacific American Journal*, 6(2).

Hannerz, Ulf. (1995). *Transnational connections: Culture, people, places*. London, New York: Routledge.

Harrison, Charles, & Wood, Paul (Eds.). (1994). *Art in theory: An anthology of changing ideas*. Oxford: Blackwell.

Hassan, Salah M. (1998). Henna mania: Body painting as a fashion statement, from tradition to Madonna. In *The art of African fashion*. Eritrea: Africa World Press.

Hesse, Gary. (2002). *Contact sheet, Alien*. Syracuse, NY: Light Work.

hooks, bell. (1992). *Black looks, race and representation*. Boston: South End Press.

Hoskote, Ranjit. (1998). Of tradition and contemporaneity. *The Art of India News Magazine*, 3(2).

Husserl, Edmund. (1965). *Ideas* (W. R. Gibson. Trans.). New York: Collier Books.

Irigaray, Luce. (1984). *An ethics of sexual difference* (Burke Carolyn and Gillian Gill, Trans.). Ithaca: Cornell University Press.

Irigaray, Luce. (1985). *Speculum of the other woman* (Gillian Gill, Trans.). Ithaca: Cornell University Press.

Jagannathan, Shakunthala. (1984). *Hinduism.* Bombay: Vakils.

Jameson, Fredric, & Masao, Miyoshi (Eds.). (1998). *The cultures of globalization.* Durham, London: Duke University Press.

Jones, Amelia. (1998). *Body art/Performing the subject.* Minneapolis, London: University of Minnesota Press.

Kakar, Sudhir. (1978). *The inner world.* New York: Oxford University Press.

Khokar, M. (1981). *Dances of India.* Madras: Vivekananda Kendra.

Kramrisch, Stella. (1955). *The art of India: Traditions of Indian sculpture, painting and architecture* (2nd ed.). London: Phaidon Press.

Kramrisch, Stella. (1981). *Manifestations of Shiva.* Philadelphia: Philadelphia Museum of Art.

Kumar, Amitava. (2002). *Bombay London New York.* London, New York: Routledge.

Kumar, Nanda Tanmaya. (2002, July 19). The Masala Bhangra girl. *India Abroad.*

Kumar, Siva R. (1999). Modern Indian art: A brief overview. *Art Journal.*

Lacan, Jacques. (1982). *Feminine sexuality* (Jaqueli Valentine M. Moghadam ne Rose, Trans.). New York: Pantheon Books.

Leeson Francis. (1962). *Kama Shilpa.* Bombay: Taraporevala Sons & Co.

Levinas, Emmanuel. (1981). *Otherwise than being or beyond essence* (Alphonso Lingis, Trans.). Pittsburgh: Duquesne University Press.

Lingis, Alphonso. (1983). *Excesses: Eros and culture.* Albany: State University of New York Press.

Lingis, Alphonso. (1985). *Libido: The French existential theories.* Bloomington: Indiana University Press.

Lingis, Alphonso. (1994). *Foreign bodies.* New York & London: Routledge.

Mani, Lata. (1998). *Contentious traditions.* Berkeley: University of California Press.

Massey, Doreen, & Jess, P. (Eds.). (1995). *A place in the world? Places, cultures and globalization.* New York: Oxford University Press.

Mazumdar. Sucheta. (1994). Moving away from a secular vision? Women, nation and cultural construction of Hindu India. In Valentine M. Moghadam (Ed.), *Identity politics and woman: Cultural reassertions and feminisms in international perspective.* Boulder, CO: Westerview Press.

Mayo, Katherine. (1927). *Mother India.* New York: Blue Ribbon Books.

McClintock, Anne. (1995). *Imperial leather race, gender and sexualities in the colonial context.* New York, London: Routledge.

Mehta, Deepa. Interview on Rediff, on the Net, movies: An Interview with Deepa Mehta, Suparn Verma; www.redfindia.com/entair/oct/24.htm.

Merleau-Ponty, Maurice. (1962). *Phenomenology of perception* (Colin Smith, Trans.). New York, London: Routledge.

Merleau-Ponty, Maurice. (1964). *The primacy of perception*. Evanston, IL: Northwestern University Press.

Mercer, Kobena. (1994). *Welcome to the jungle*. New York & London: Routledge.

Mickunas, Algis. (1993). Cultural logics and the search for national identities. In *Phenomenology of the cultural disciplines*. Netherlands: Kluwer Academic Publishers.

Mickunas, Algis (n. d.). The cosmic traces. Unpublished article, presented at the Husserl Circle, Ohio University.

Minh-ha, Trinh T. (1989). *Woman, native, other*. Bloomington: Indiana University Press.

Minh-ha, Trinh T. (1999). *Cinema interval*. London, New York: Routledge.

Mitter, Partha. (1977). *Much maligned monsters*. Oxford: Clarendon Press.

Mitter, Partha. (1994). *Art and nationalism in colonial India 1850–1922*. Cambridge: Cambridge University Press.

Mookerjee, Ajit. (1982). *Kundalini*. London: Thames and Hudson.

Mookerjee, Ajit. (1985). *Ritual art of India*. London: Thames and Hudson.

Mookherjee, Ajit. (1988). *Kali, the feminine force*. London: Thames and Hudson.

Moorehouse, Geoffrey. (1974). *Calcutta*. Harmondsworth.

Mukerjee, Radhakamal. (1964). *The flowering of Indian art*. London: Asia Publishing House.

Mukherjee, Radhakamal. (1965). *The cosmic art of India*. Bombay, New Delhi: Allied Publishers.

Muller, Buhler. (Trans.). (1964). *The laws of Manu*. Delhi: Motilal Banarasidas.

Murthy, Anantha. (1998). Why not worship in the nude? Reflections of a novelist in his time. In Fred Dallmayr and G. N. Devy (Eds.), *Between tradition and modernity: India's search for identity*. London & New Delhi: Altamira Press.

Nadkarni, Dnyaneshwar. (1996). *Hussain riding the lightning*. Bombay: Popular Prakashan.

Nandagopal. C. (1997, December). *Hindu Folio*.

Narayan, Uma. (1997). *Dislocating cultures*. New York: Routledge.

National Gallery of Modern Art. (1997). *Contemporary Indian paintings*. New Delhi: India.

Nead, Lynda. (1995). *Chila Kumari Burman: Beyond two cultures*. London: Kala Press.

Neret, Gilles. (1993). *Erotic Art* (Muthesius Angeika & Riernschneider Burhard, Eds.). Italy: Benedikt Taschen.

Nietzsche, Friedrich. (1967). *The birth of tragedy* (Walter Kaufmann, Ed.). New York: Random House.

Nietzsche, Friedrich. (1968). *The will to power* (Walter Kaufman, Trans.). New York: Vintage Books.

Oomen, T. K. (1997). *Citizenship and national identity. From colonialism to globalism*. London, New York: Routledge.

O'Flaherty, Wendy Doninger (Ed.). (1980). *Karma and the rebirth in classical traditions*. Berkeley: University of California Press.

Pal. Pratapaditya. *The sensuous immortals*. Cambridge, London: MIT Press.

Panikkar, Shivaji. (1999). *Creative process*. Bombay: The Guild Art Gallery.

Parry, Benita. (1987). Problems in current theories of colonial discourse. *Oxford Literary Review*, 9.

Parry, Benita. (1998). *Delusions and discoveries*. London, New York: Verso.

Pfeil, Fred. (1994). No Basta Teorizar: In-difference to solidarity in contemporary fiction, theory and practice. In Inderpal Grewal and Caren Kaplan (Eds.), *Scattered hegemonies: Postmodernity and transnational feminist practices*. Minneapolis: University of Minnesota Press.

Philip, Nourbese. (1997). *A genealogy of resistance*. Canada: The Mercury Press.

Pinney, Christopher. (1995). Moral topophilia: The significations of landscape in Indian oleographs. In E. Hirsch and M. O'Hanlon (Eds.), *The anthropology of landscape perspectives on place and space*. Oxford, New York: Oxford University Press.

Pundole Art Gallery: Bombay (1995). *Mithunas*. Bombay: India.

Puri, Jyothi. (1999). *Woman, body, desire in post-colonial India*. New York: Routledge.

Radhakrishnan, Sarvepalli. (1923). *Indian philosophy* (2 vols.). London: G. Allen and Unwin.

Radhakrisnan, Sarvepalli. (1937). *The individual in east and west*. London: Oxford University Press.

Radhakrishnan, Sarvepalli. (Trans.). (1953). *The principal Upanishads*. New York Harper.

Ramachandran, R.P. (1979). *The Indian philosophy of beauty* (2 vols.). Madras: University of Madras.

Rawson, Philip. (1977). *Erotic art of India*. London: Thames & Hudson.

Rawson, Philip. (1981). *Oriental erotic art*. London, New York: Quartet Books.

Robertson, Roland. (1992). *Globalization: Social theory and global culture*. Newbury Park, CA: Sage.

Rowland, Benjamin. (1953). *Art and architecture of India*. Delhi: Penguin Books.

Said, Edward. (1978). *Orientalism*. Harmondsworth: Penguin.

Said, Edward. (1993). *Culture and imperialism*. New York: Alfred Knoff.

Sarcar, Anjali. (1997). India's art in transition. *Hindu Folio*.

Sharma, Parvez. (1999). Burning down the house. *Trikone Magazine*.

Sharp, H., (1923). *Selections from Educational Records*, Vol. 1. Calcutta: Superintendent, Govt. Printing India.

Sinari, Ramakant. (1970). *The structure of Indian thought*. Springfield, IL: Charles C. Thomas Publishers.

Sinha, Gayatri. (1996). *Expressions and evocations: Contemporary women artists of India*. Bombay: Marg Publications.

Sirhandi, Marcella. (1999). Manipulating cultural idioms. *CAA Art Journal*.

Sloterdijk, Peter. (1987). *Critique of cynical reason* (Michael Eldred, Trans.). Minneapolis: University of Minnesota Press.

Spivak, Gayatri Chakravorty. (1986). Imperialism and sexual difference. *Oxford Literary Review*, 8(1–2)

Spivak, Gayatri Chakravorty. (1986). Three women's texts and a critique of imperialism. In Henry Louis Gates (Ed.), *Race writing and difference*. Chicago: University of Chicago Press.

Spivak, Gayatri Chakravorty. (1988). Can the subaltern speak. In Cary Nelson & Lawrence Grossberg (Eds.), *Marxism and interpretation of culture*. Urbana: University of Illinois Press.

Spivak, Gayatri Chakravorty. (1999). *A critique of postcolonial reason*. Cambridge, London: Harvard University Press.

Subramanyan. K.G. (1987). *The living tradition*. Calcutta: Seagull Books.

Stanton, C. Domna. (1989). Difference on trial. In Jeffner Allen & Marion Iris Young (Eds.), *The thinking muse*. Bloomington, Indianapolis: Indiana University Press.

Tambiah, Yasmin. (1993). Decolonization and third world lesbian identities. Paper presented at the Seminar on the History of Alternative Sexualities, New Delhi.

Thadani, Giti. (1996). *Sakhiyani*. London: Cassell.

Thapar, Suruchi (1993). Woman as activist; woman as symbols: A study of the Indian Nationalist Movement. *Feminist Review, 44*.

Tharu, Susie, & Lalita, K. (Eds.). (1991). *Women writing in India 600 B.C. to the present* (Vol 1 and Vol 2). New York: The Feminist Press.

Verma, Nirmal. (1998). India and Europe—Some reflections on self and other. In Fred Dallmayr & G. N. Devy (Eds.), *Between tradition and modernity: India's search for identity*. London & New Delhi: Altamira Press.

Vivekananda. (1963). *Complete works* (Vol. 2). Calcutta.

Viswanathan, Gauri. (1989). *Masks of conquest*. New York: Columbia University Press.

Williams, Patrick, & Chrisman, Laura. (1994). *Colonial discourse and post-colonial theory*. New York: Columbia University Press.

Yegenoglu, Meyda. (1998). *Colonial fantasies*. Cambridge: Cambridge University Press.

Young, Robert. (1990). *White mythologies, writing history and the West*. London, New York: Routledge.

Young, Robert. (1995). *Colonial desire: Hybridity in theory, culture and race*. London and New York: Routledge.

Zimmer, Heinrich. (1947). *Myths and symbols in Indian art and civilizations*. New York: Pantheon Books.

Zimmer, Heinrich. (1951). *Philosophies of India*. New York: Pantheon Books.

Sanskrit Texts

Agni Purana

Arthashastra

Atharva Veda

Aithareya Brahmanya

Amritabindu Upanishad

Bhagavadgita

Bhagavata Purana

Brihad Aranyaka Upanishad

Chandoga Upanishad
Devibhagvata Purana
Devi Upanishad
Gandharva Tantra
Kali Tantra
Kamasutra of Vatsyana
Koka Shastra
Lakshmi Tantra
Linga Purana
Mahabharata
Maitri.Upanishad
Matsya Purana
Mundaka Upanishad
Ramayana
Rig Veda
The Laws of Manu
Vatula Shudda Agma
Yoni Tantra

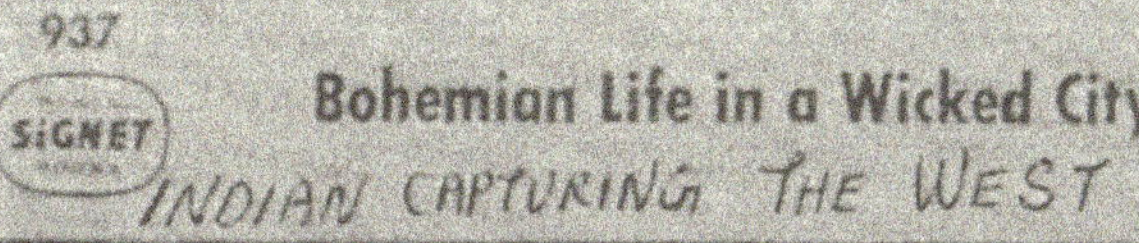
937
SiGNET
Bohemian Life in a Wicked City
INDIAN CAPTURING THE WEST
Goodbye to
INDIA
by
MENON
KENNA
A SIGNET BOOK
Complete and Unabridged

Author Index

Ackerly, J.R., 52(n80), *103*
Alvarez, L., 72(n106), *103*
Anzaldua, G., 1(n1), 42(n66), *103*

Banaji, S., 60(n85), *103*
Berry, C., 67(n103–105), *103*
Bharucha, R., 17(n34–36), *104*
Boman-Behram, B.K., 23(n44), *104*

Chandra, S., 24(n47), *104*
Chapkis, W., 25(n49–51), *104*
Chatterjee, P., 63(n100), *104*
Chopra, S., 47(n75–76), *104*
Cunningham, A., 29(n38), 52(n79), *104*

Derrida, J., 6(n19, n21), *104*
Dunning, J., 16(n31, n33), *104*

Ebin, V., 43(n67), *104*

Fanon, F., 91(n107), *105*
Foucault, M., 7(n22), *105*
Frazer, W., 23(n43), *105*

Gandhi, M., 63(n98), *105*
Guillermo, G., 41(n64), *105*

Hassan, S.M., 43(n68–69), 44(n70–71), 46(n72), 47(n73), 54(n83), *105*
Hesse, G., 32(n56), *105*
Hooks, b., 47(n77), *105*

Kakar, S., 63(n102), *106*
Khokar, M., 14(n29–30), *106*
Kumar, A., 61(n86–87), *106*
Kumar, N.T., 18(n37), *106*

Lalita, K., 22(n39), 23(n40–42), *109*
Levinas, 6(n20), *106*

Martin, F., 67(n103–105), *103*
Mayo, K., 23(n45), *106*
Mazumbar, S., 63(n99), *106*
Mercer, K., 53(n82), *106*
Mickunas, A., 12(n24), 37(n63), *107*
Minh-ha, T., 1(n1), 42(n65), *107*
Moorehouse, G., 50(n78), *107*
Muller, B., 62(n95), *107*

Nandagopal, C., 13(n25–26), 14(n27–28), *107*
Nead, L., 29(n53–55), *107*

Parry, B., 52(n80–81), *108*
Pfeil, F., 55(n84), *108*
Philip, M.N., 8(n23), *108*
Pinney, C., 28(n52), *108*
Puri, J., 35(n61), *108*

Sharma, P., 34(n60), *108*
Sharp, H., 23(43), *108*

Tambiah, Y., 62(n93), *109*
Thadani, G., 61(n88–90), 62(n92), *109*
Thapar, S., 63(n96–97, n101), *109*
Tharu, S., 22(n39), 23(n40–42), *109*

Verma, N., 2(n3), 3(n4–7), 4(n8–11), 5(n12–14), 6(n15–18), *109*
Vivekananda, 61(n91), 62(n94), *109*

Young, R., 6(n20), *109*
Yue, A., 67(n103–105), *103*

Subject Index

Adivasis (untouchables), 35
aesthetics:
  "classical," 48
  colonization and, 49
  framing and, 48
  of globalization, 89
  of Hindu art, 20
  identity and, 365
  Indian, 19, 24, 43, 49–50, 55
  Other and, 7
  purity and, 11
  of postcolonialism, 7
  race and, 29, 48–49
  senses and, 43–44
  traditions and, 48–50, 60, 63
adya shakti (maternal force), 50, 61–62,
  64
agamic, 13
angabhoga, 13–14
Angika, 16–17
arts of the Other:
  appropriation and, 42, 44, 47, 53, 55,
    68
  disruption and, 14, 17, 47–56
  as erotic, 1–2, 4, 19–36, 52, 66
  as exotic, 1–2, 4, 17–19, 29, 34,
    41–44, 47–48, 50–56, 89
  as natural rather than art, 53
  as primitive, 2, 5–6, 34, 41–43, 47,
    54–55
  rearticulation of, 48
  suppression of, 14, 17, 35, 42, 48
  as trendy, 17–18, 42–44

Aryan heritage, 61
Asian imaginaries, 67
atman (self), 4

being in the world, a, 1
bhakti (tradition or essence), 14
bhangra, 18, 54
Bharat Mata (motherland), 63
Bharata, 17
Bhogastree, 14
Black faith, 49
body:
  as battleground, 1
  as canvas, 44
  coextensive with the environment, 1
  cosmic, 16–17
  judgment and, 11–12
  as property, 1
  as site of knowledge and power, 1
body art, 42–48, 53–55
Bollywood, 18, 31–32, 60, 64, 66
border culture, 42
Brahman, 4, 12, 35, 50
brahamanic tradition, 61
British and Great Britain:
  assimilation with, 5–6, 23–24
  Chaudhari on, 3–4
  Chiplunkar on, 24
  colonization of India by, 2, 4, 22–24
  Devadasi system abolished by, 14
  "dirtiness" and, 2
  enlightened rationalism of, 3
  Ghar-Vapasi and, 35–36

British and Great Britain: (*continued*)
  Indians' encounter with, 3–4
  Kali and, 49–50
  maternal force and, 61–63
  moralizing of, 20, 23, 48, 52, 65–66

Calcutta, 50
Chandralekha, 15–17
Chiplunkar, 24
Christianity, 35–36
classical aesthetics, 48
cosmic presence, 12–18
cultural appropriation, 42, 44, 47, 53,
    55, 68
cultural homogenization, 26–27, 41, 52

dance, 12–18, 38, 42, 48
death of knowing, 66–67, 72–73
desire, 53–54, 89
Devadasi system, 13–14, 17
devas, 13
dharma (righteousness), 4–5, 66
Dhobi Ghat, 84
diasporas, 17–18, 31, 37, 60, 67
difference, 1, 25, 37, 49, 53, 56, 66
disruption, 14, 17, 47–56

Earth, 65–66
English language, 3, 24–25, 28, 30, 60
eroticism, 1–2, 4, 12, 19–36, 52, 66
ethics and morality, 1–2, 4, 6–7, 12,
    19–23, 36–37, 42–43, 48, 52–53,
    60–65
Eurocentrism, 49
European scholars on the Other, 7
excess, 11–12, 19, 52, 64, 80
exoticism, 1–2, 4, 17–19, 29, 34, 41–44,
    47–48, 50–56, 89

fashion, 25–26, 42–44, 47–48, 54
femininity, 2, 17, 29, 43, 61–66
film, 15, 18, 28, 31–32, 34–35, 50, 54,
    60–61, 64–66, 91
Fire, 34–35, 65

Gandhi, Mahatma, 35, 55, 62–63, 66, 82

gender:
  colonialism and, 12, 20, 23, 52
  dance and, 12–18
  identity and, 61–62
Ghar-Vapasi, 35
Ghora Angrez, 76
Global Space, 89
globalization: 36–38, 41–43, 66
  aesthetics of, 89
  art and, 19
  Bollywood and, 66
  desire and, 89
  destructiveness of, 28
  identity and, 36–38, 89
  of Indian marriages, 66–68, 72
  logic of, 3, 24, 26, 41
  morality and, 19, 42–43
  reflective, 36–37
  superiority and, 42
goddess images and stereotypes, 20, 29,
    49–51, 61, 63
Great Britain. *See* British and Great
    Britain
Guru, 91

henna body art, 42–48, 53–55
Hermeneutics, 34–35, 48, 53
heterosexuality, 34, 61–62
Hindu fundamentalists/fanatics, 21–22,
    34–36, 65
Hinduism, 3–6, 20–22, 28–36, 44,
    65–66, 68
Hollywood, 18, 46, 50, 53
Hussain, M. F., 31–32

identity:
  ambiguity of, 89
  Burman and, 30–31
  body decoration and, 43
  body politic of, 11
  compacting of, 37
  diasporas and, 37, 67
  difference and, 37
  discovered, 38
  ethnic, 18, 89
  gender and, 61–62

globalization and questions of, 36–38, 89
Hindu, 4, 36, 61
lesbian, 34–35
Matthew and, 31
national, 3, 26, 60
passports and, 29–30
personal, 36–37
self-display images and, 29
technology and, 67–68
immigrant space, 41
in-between, 36, 93
in-between space, 6–7
Indian Space, 26, 42, 54–55. *See also* Third Space
Indiana Jones and the Temple of Doom, 50
Indianness, 18, 51, 60–63, 84

Jain, Sarina, 18, 54
jazz, 48

Kali, 29, 35, 49–51, 63–64
kama (love), 12, 19–20, 22, 34–35, 65
kamic (eros), 2, 12, 19, 24, 35, 52
Karma, 36
Khajuraho, 13, 19–20, 22, 34, 51–52, 86
Kunhiraman, Kanayi, 20–21
kshatriya tradition, 61

Laws of Manu, 62
lesbian identity, 34–35
lila (desire), 20, 65
liberation, 32, 89

Madonna, 44–47
Mahabharata, 35
marginal space, 42
marriage and weddings:
    arranged, 32, 67–68, 72
    assisted arranged, 72
    body decoration and, 43–44, 47
    newspaper advertisements for, 68
    technology and, 67–68
Masala Bhangra, 18
masculinity, 5, 61–63, 66
materialism, 3, 37, 47, 61–63

matrika (mother), 61. *See also* mother and motherhood
McDonalds, 77
Mithunas, 19, 51
mobility, 38, 54, 67–68, 72
moksha, 4–5
money, 1, 60
Monsoon Wedding, 54
mother and motherhood, 20, 43, 50, 61–66, 72
Muddupalani, 22–23
music, 14, 17, 42, 48, 54
Muslims, 3–4, 21–22, 37, 44, 66–68

nationalism, 3, 60–63, 65
native/natives, 23, 34, 52–53, 84
naturalness, 24
nautch, 12–14
nudity and naked bodies, 1, 4, 11, 21–22, 29

objectified, 1–2, 7, 11–12, 21–22, 52–53
Otherness/Othering, 3–4, 41–42, 53, 56. *See also* art of the Other
outsourcing, 90

parmatma, 4
patriarchy, 14, 17, 29, 34, 61–65
patriotism, 60
phallocentrism, 53
photography, 32–34
poetry, 15–16, 22–24, 54
politics, 1, 6–7, 11, 18, 21–23, 28, 34–36, 51, 54, 63, 65
Prakurti, 16
Prince, 46
prostitution, 12–14, 17, 51
psychologization, 11–12, 23
purity, 11, 60–62
Purusa, 16

Radhika Santwanam, 22–23
Raga, 15
rangabhoga, 13–14

reclothing, 1, 7, 42, 56
redressing/disrobing, 1, 4, 11, 42, 47, 51,
    56, 59
Rickshaw ride, 78

sadism, 1–2, 7
salt *Satyagraha*, 63
Saraswati, 21–22
Sartre, Jean-Paul, 7, 91
scarification, 42–44, 48
sculpture, 19–21, 42, 49, 51–52
Seduction, 2, 7, 51–52, 59–61, 66, 89
seductive space, 7, 90
self, 1–7
self-colonization, 51
self-creation, 67
self-deportation, 90–91
self-image, colonizer's, 7
self-inscription, 67
self-portraits, 29
self-referentiality, 53–54
self-rule, Indian, 63
Sex Goddess, 51
Shakti, 20, 35, 49–50, 61–65
Sharira Mandala, 17
Shirin Neshat, 53
Shiva, 17, 35
Shivalingam, 16, 76
Sita, 32, 34, 61–63
speed-dating, 67–68, 72
spiritual East, 61–63
Sprinkle, Annie, 51
Sting, 46

Subjectified/subjectivation, 11–12, 14,
    19–20, 42–43
suppression, 14, 17, 35, 42, 48
Swami (Lord), 14

taal (Indian beat), 18, 54, 60
tattoos, 42, 44, 48
technology, marriage and, 67–68
terrorism, 34, 60
Third Space, 26, 41–42, 56
Third World, 41–42, 89–91
tradition and modernity, 60–61
transgression, 11–13, 17, 34, 42–43,
    50–53, 66
translation as interpretation, 41

Upanishad, 10

Vedic tradition, 3, 14, 16, 6
victimization, 3, 7–8, 14, 17, 62, 89–91
Victorian, 34, 65
virya (manhood), 61

Western space, 41–42
Westernization, 4–6, 32, 60–64
Whiteness, 6, 23, 25–26, 44, 47, 49,
    52–55, 89–90
Who am I, 56, 60, 87
Who are we, 36–38
Who we are, 36, 91

Yakshi, 20–21

Zen Mehndi evenings, 46